WORLD WAR II
in
NORTH STATE
CALIFORNIA

WORLD WAR II
in
NORTH STATE CALIFORNIA

Al M. Rocca

THE
History
PRESS

Published by The History Press
Charleston, SC
www.historypress.com

Opposite: Author's father-in-law, Gene S. Tanno. *Author's collection.*

First published 2023

Manufactured in the United States

ISBN 9781467154635

Library of Congress Control Number: 2023938595

I dedicate this book to the courageous men and women of the northern counties that comprise the Sacramento Valley (North State) who served in the military and on the civilian home front. Those selfless men and women dedicated their lives for three and a half years to produce the crops and materials needed here in the North State, throughout California and the entire nation, participating in local and regional defense organizations, buying war bonds and helping each other deal with the stress and challenges of a wartime economy and environment.

Personally, I would like to highlight the tremendous act of valor of my father-in-law, Gene S. Tanno, for his courage at the Battle of the Bulge in World War II, earning a Bronze Star for putting himself at risk during his rescuing of fifty-five American soldiers stranded behind enemy lines. After safely driving through snow-clogged roads with the first group of rescued men, he selflessly volunteered to go back for the remaining contingent of soldiers.

CONTENTS

ACKNOWLEDGEMENTS

I am grateful to the many regional organizations that supplied photographs and content that made this book possible. Each county historical society and library revealed a deep commitment to help share the region's rich history, specifically its county's contribution to the war effort. I want to thank Carol Mieske of the Tehama County Genealogical & Historical Society for giving me a tour of its new, ultramodern facilities tucked away in the Tehama County Library in Red Bluff. Thanks to her impressive knowledge and organization, she quickly found relevant materials and photographs of the period, uncovering a key source concerning the U.S. Navy's participation in setting up a naval airfield in Red Bluff in 1944. She also provided 35mm rolls of the Red Bluff *Daily News*. I also want to thank the many local North State librarians who provided access to the 35mm film records of newspapers covering the years 1941–45.

I want to thank the librarians at the Marysville Yuba County Library in particular for taking time to show me their new online access to their historical newspaper documents. The new system allows complete access from remote locations, such as your home, to a wide number of Yuba County newspapers dating back many years. Special thanks go to the librarians at the Butte County location for coordinating my multiple requests for interlibrary loan material of 35mm film of historic newspapers from libraries throughout the North State. I also would like to recognize David Nopel of the Chico History Museum for his assistance in locating and providing photographs from the 1943 Chico High School yearbook and other sources.

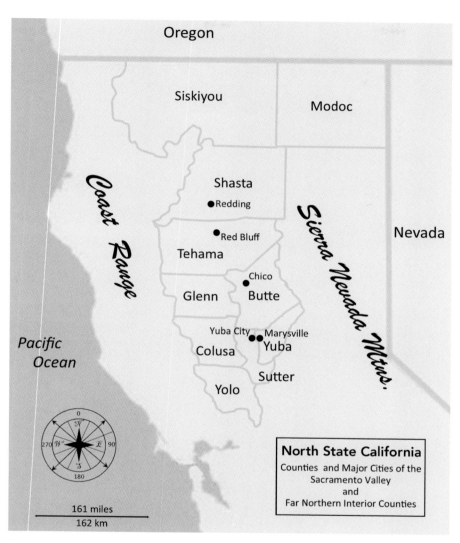

Oregon

Siskiyou

Modoc

Coast Range

Shasta
●Redding

●Red Bluff
Tehama

Nevada

Sierra Nevada Mtns.

Chico
●
Glenn   Butte

Yuba City ● ● Marysville
Colusa   Yuba
Pacific
Ocean
Sutter

Yolo

0
270 W°   E° 90
180

161 miles
162 km

North State California
Counties and Major Cities of the
Sacramento Valley
and
Far Northern Interior Counties

Author's collection.

INTRODUCTION

There is no misuse of the often-heard demographic description "the Greatest Generation." Their patience, determination and outright courage allowed them to survive and thrive through two of the most consequential periods in American history, the Great Depression and World War II. The giddy wild days of money and plenty of the 1920s disappeared in late October 1929, immediately resulting in massive labor layoffs, business bankruptcies and a creeping rise in crime and general hopelessness. The North State, despite rumors to the contrary in the eastern portion of the United States, did not thrive economically during the ensuing decade. Hardships prevailed as national politics played out, kicking out Herbert Hoover and ushering in Franklin D. Roosevelt and his liberal reconstruction of federal power, known collectively as the New Deal—power to create new agencies designed to get people working, no matter the debt incurred or the traditions broken. Meanwhile, in the small three-room bungalow houses located at the edge of any North State city limits—the home, kept clean, inside and out, with just enough of a backyard for two children to play comfortably—lived families: husband and wife, with kids, a boy and a girl, the children separated in age by three years, the adults tested in body and spirit, having struggled through eleven years of a ghastly economic downturn, looking hopefully yet realistically to the future.

During the Depression years, agencies like the Works Progress Administration (WPA), Office of Price Administration (OPA) and the Public Works Administration (PWA)—the latter providing funding for bridges, dams and airports, among other noteworthy new projects, expansions or renovations—expanded programs for immediate economic relief. Some of the work projects in the North State included Bidwell Park improvements, Bidwell Bowl Amphitheater (Chico), Biggs City Hall (Butte County), a bus garage for Marysville High School, road paving for Route 20 in Marysville, Chico Municipal Airport, Citrus Elementary School (Chico), Silver Dollar Fairgrounds (Chico), Redding Post Office, Redding Fire House, Veterans Memorial Building (Redding), Yuba City Hall and more.

With farming a prime economic force in the North State counties, the Depression resulted in tough times, forcing growers to make desperate financial decisions as the crisis deepened throughout the 1930s. Wages in California for farm-related work dropped from $3.50 to $1.90 per day; later, to fight the flood of incoming state workers, a three-year residency requirement disqualified most farm workers from government relief. Yet the farmers survived, crops were produced and small business owners did their best to carry on. Some made it successfully, while others did not; everyone waited for better times to arrive.

On December 7, 1941, everything changed. The next morning, President Roosevelt asked Congress for a declaration of war against Japan, followed days later by additional declarations against Italy and Germany. This would be a world war, a marshaling of everyone in the country, fundamentally and dramatically changing an individual's relationship with his or her government, beginning with the city and county entities and quickly moving to state and national responsibilities. Every North State resident, young or old, healthy or otherwise, now became part of a gigantic mobilization of people and resources, with national officials expecting the North State to play a vital role. Men, and later women, needed to enlist in the army, navy or coast guard; the Selective Training and Service Act of 1940 already required men between the ages of twenty-one and forty-five to register for the draft. This was America's first peacetime draft, but everyone knew that war appeared inevitable.

This book investigates how the war affected North State residents, beginning with the shocking news of the attack on Pearl Harbor and its immediate aftermath. Resentment toward Japanese Americans or Japanese nationals then residing in the North State resulted in the rounding up of these residents and their relocation to the Marysville Assembly Center; life in the center, though only a few weeks in length, proved disheartening and debilitating. The military, expecting Japanese air attacks and a possible land invasion somewhere along the northern coast of California, set up a system of army and navy airfields and base camps. No sooner had the war begun than the government requested its citizens, all of them, to support the war effort by regularly buying war bonds, and the North State responded well to those efforts, in some cases surpassing quotas and goals.

This book takes a close look at how America's national policies of rationing food, tires, gas, metal and many other items played out with nervous and curious North State residents, especially at the beginning of the conflict. Additionally, we survey the types of entertainment available to citizens, young and old, including movies, radio programs and newspapers. The largest single project dominating the North State during the war was the continuing construction of the mighty Shasta Dam. Designed to store a huge amount of water that would, in turn, power the four large turbines from which electricity traveled to a variety of locations in the south—most notably, the burgeoning war industries in the Bay Area—Shasta Dam gained national attention. Starting in 1938, construction engineers faced constant physical, environmental and worker challenges throughout the war years 1941–45. Elsewhere around the North State, numerous men and women displayed a high level of patriotism and heroism during World War II; one chapter of this book summarizes some of their courageous stories, military and civilian alike. I hope you enjoy reading about the many North State people and events that contributed to America's victory in World War II— our greatest generation.

Chapter 1

PEARL HARBOR AND

ITS AFTERMATH

The Attack and the North State's Reaction

The initial firestorm of reaction to the Japanese attack on Pearl Harbor spread quickly, consuming each North State citizen in different ways, possibly the result of the air bombardment being a "sneak attack," possibly the result of their understanding of what it meant to their future. While Chico city residents huddled around their family radio consoles on December 7 hearing, for the first time, of the Japanese attack on Pearl Harbor, *Chico Enterprise* reporters, typesetters and other staff worked feverishly to gather the flood of news stories pouring in throughout the day. The following day, the newspaper, sporting one of the largest font sizes in its inventory, succinctly proclaimed, "U.S. Declares War." The front page covered the international situation, alarming residents about the seriousness of Japanese aggression, noting a rapid, devastating attack on Manila, a major city in the Philippines. Already, rumors were circulating in the Bay Area, Los Angeles and San Diego that the West Coast of America was next—the invasion might occur anywhere along California's long coastline, the North State included.

Chico's citizens reacted patriotically. Mrs. James Wright declared, "We must all do our part," realizing that all North State residents needed to help the war effort. Carl Fanno knew what this moment meant for all able-bodied men when he simply said, "There is only one thing to do," referring to an expected call for military volunteers. Frank Enlow tried to understand why Japan would want a war with America: "They [the Japanese] were foolish to mess with the United States." "There is no reason for me to form an opinion,"

The Japanese attack on Pearl Harbor devastated the United States Pacific Fleet. This photo was taken from a Japanese airplane during the attack. *Library of Congress.*

Herbert Simpson demurred, understanding that events were unfolding too rapidly to fully comprehend the situation. However, most North State residents believed that all-out war now existed, probably best summarized by Fred Coekler, who said, "After this shocking attack there is only one policy to follow." Mrs. Olive Pearl excitedly exclaimed, "We are all ready to fight," suggesting her community's willingness to participate actively in whatever function the federal, state and local governments deemed necessary.

All day long on Monday afternoon, December 8, citizens met in groups on downtown street corners to hear the latest news and conjecture the next steps. The newspaper reported the city was "in turmoil," mad about the attack, confused as to what was actually happening overseas and here on the west coast of California and yearning to do something, anything. Already, young men were reporting downtown anxious to enlist: Chico State College students, high school students of age (eighteen) and "young businessmen," among them more than a few overexcited under-eighteen-year-old teenagers. This same scenario played out on the downtown streets of Redding, Marysville and other towns throughout the North State. A navy recruiter, already stationed on the second floor of the Chico Post Office, answered hundreds of questions about the induction process, while Marie Trapp, clerk of the local draft board, made it clear that only young men eighteen or over and "absolutely physically" fit would be considered for active service. On the other hand, the federal law restricting upper-age enlistment to thirty-eight years old became a hot topic of debate at an emergency meeting of the local draft board, with the board president, Grayson Price, believing a repeal of that law, allowing older candidates to enter military service, was imminent.

The enlistment age, set at eighteen years of age, prompted all young men to register immediately after their birthday. Jack LaBarre, Shasta County clerk, notified local newspapers of those young men, announcing their names and communities. This practice continued throughout much of the war, with the expectation that no one need induce these young men to do their duty. Loaded as "contingents" onto buses around the North State, the eighteen-year-old men shipped out at regular intervals to Sacramento, where comprehensive physical examinations occurred. During this process, new recruits learned they would receive a military classification determination that would decide their future with the army or navy. The classification, complex as it was, organized status into four "Class" sections: Class 1, available for military service; Class 2, deferred because of occupation; Class 3, deferred because of dependency; and Class 4, unacceptable for military service.

On top of the predominant categories—such as I-A, nominally available for military service; II-B, deferred in war production; III-A, deferred for dependency; and IV-B, public official deferred by law—numerous subcategories fleshed out nooks for special circumstances. Some of these situations included: I-A-O, nominally available for noncombat military service (conscientious objector); II-C, deferred for agriculture; III-D (H), deferred by reason of extreme hardship and privation to wife, child or parent, age thirty-eight to forty-four, inclusive (added in April 1943); and IV-C, any registrant, whether a national of the United States or an alien, who, because of his nationality or ancestry, was within a class of persons not acceptable to armed forces or the director of Selective Service for work of national importance.[1]

Meanwhile, local citizens, nervous about the possible immediate threat of military invasion, met to discuss organizational and procedural contingencies. The American Legion, Chico Post No. 17, discussed a variety of actions, including blackout security patrols so as not to alert Japanese pilots of possible targets and the creation of a network of aircraft

Local newspapers such as the *Redding Record-Searchlight* announced the Japanese attack on Pearl Harbor, covering the disastrous event with second editions as more details became available. *Library of Congress.*

observation posts. Officials finally agreed to maintain over thirty posts in Butte County initially and add more later as needed; these "posts" would operate on a twenty-four-hour cycle, with observers coming and going based on their available time. This action started immediately on December 8.

On another front, efforts began at once to protect already established "defense school property." This included "defense classrooms at the [Chico] high school" and the flight instruction headquarters on Broadway Street. Nervous more about sabotage than airplane attack, B.W. Shaper, supervisor of defense training in the region, emphasized the need to protect the thousands of dollars of money invested in operational equipment, warning that "sabotage protection" would become "a major defense task." His words rang loud and clear. Soon anyone looking Japanese would come under suspicion.

For some North State residents, worrying about the fate of service members and their families began the day after Pearl Harbor. Mrs. William Stuke, office manager at the local Chico branch of AAA, became concerned when she learned that Hickham Airfield, near Honolulu, had come under a Japanese attack. Stuke believed her brother, Lieutenant James Keefer, remained safe with his ship, a minesweeper vessel. Officials indicated to Stuke that they believed her husband William's ship to be at sea during the raid, but Keefer's wife and their newborn child lived in accommodations quite near the airfield. Reports flooded in all day describing the vast destruction of airplanes, hangars and nearby civilian buildings as Japanese planes bombed and strafed aggressively. News did reach Woodland, California, that First Lieutenant Hans Christiansen, a marine aviator stationed at Pearl Harbor, died in action; he was twenty-one.

Corporal Harold Johanson, a North State native, just happened to be on leave visiting his parents. A pilot by training, Johanson spent a few hours with family, then quickly returned to Hamilton Field at Novato, California, a major training and staging area for the First Wing of the Army Air Corps. Tragically, a squadron of B-17 bombers from Hamilton Field flew across the Pacific, approached Hickman Field on December 7 and was mistakenly shot down while attempting to land. It is not known if Johanson served on any of those planes. For much of the remainder of the war, Hamilton Airfield monitored air traffic for the Bay Area and North State.

Yuba County's first war fatality was Harold (Cotton) McCutcheon, a young naval enlistment; he saw action and became an early victim of the Pearl Harbor attack. When news reached Yuba County weeks later, seven of McCutcheon's friends living in Gridley and Biggs moved quickly to enlist. McCutcheon's tenure in the navy proved brief; he had enlisted only months before. Stories such as this instilled a new reality of life in the North State: young men faced the ultimate challenge of human survival once sent into a war zone, Pearl Harbor being first.

One of the first North State residents to learn of their son's fate was Shasta County resident J.S. Ross. Working as a warehouseman on the Shasta Dam project, Ross and his wife knew their son, Donald, twenty-one years old and a private first class, worked in and around the naval base at Pearl Harbor, guarding a bridge. Only a couple of days after the attack, the Ross family received a cablegram from the War Department explaining their son was a "casualty," leaving open not only the hope of his survival but also the distressing possibility that Donald had received debilitating wounds. However, one local resident informed Ross that receiving a cablegram so soon after an attack usually meant "killed in action." No subsequent report appeared in the local newspaper to verify the fate of Donald Ross.

By the hundreds, North State residents tried in vain to send or request word of family or friends stationed or living on Oahu Island or on other islands of the Hawaiian archipelago. The government quickly put the word out that priority messaging remained open only for military exchanges; officials would not accept or honor personal requests for an indefinite period. Soon, rumors abounded that Japanese forces might strike the Pacific Island of Wake. Frank Crowe, superintendent in charge of the construction of Shasta Dam, now worried as his nephew Frank Crowe Jr. worked for the Morrison-Knudsen Company constructing defense works on that island—no contact permitted. Redding citizen Carmel Rogers reported that his son Clifford served on the battleship *Pennsylvania*, which Japanese sources reported as "sinking"—it actually received only a single bomb strike, suffering only minimal damage, sitting in dry dock, safe from Japanese torpedoes. Meanwhile, Mrs. W.W. Ball, who had recently returned to Shasta County from Manila in the Philippines with her daughter, Barbara, stressed over the safety of her husband, who remained stationed near the capital city. For days, North State newspapers reported the names of local residents with family or friends living within the "War Zone" from Midway Island in the north to the Philippines in the south and, of course, any of the Hawaiian Islands; everyone waited for any bit of information, glued to each radio announcement or latest edition of the local newspaper.

When asked about their views on the war news for the *Redding Record-Searchlight*, North State residents did not hold back. One citizen, furious over the Japanese's duplicity of pretending to negotiate peace in Washington, D.C., while the Pearl Harbor attack commenced, ranted, "Well, I guess we will have to go over and get us some Japanese." One older resident mused, "I wish I was back in my old outfit. My buddies and I were stationed just five miles from Manila." Optimistically, Harold Walsh announced, "The war will be over in just three months." Harry Vartholomoes thought otherwise: "We're in this thing for at least three years. It's going to be a tough war." Vartholomoes was proven right; the war was destined to linger on for over three years, with tough consequences for those fighting overseas and those fighting on the home front, supplying America's growing war machine. Another Shasta County resident predicted, "They'll have us all in the army yet"; this proved true, as the call for action and involvement began immediately.

Expecting hostilities for months, the U.S. Army Air Corps set up fourteen thousand coastal observation posts on the Atlantic and Pacific coasts, where volunteers made naked eye and binocular scans of local skies, searching

Posters such as this one soon began appearing in North State newspapers and regional and national magazines. By July 1942, 142,613 young men had enlisted in the Marine Corps, 7,138 officers and 135,475 enlisted men. *Library of Congress.*

for aircraft. The North State, being close to the Pacific coastline, sprouted numerous observation posts and local "filter centers" where observers called in to report a sighting. One major filter center existed in Redding, and just days after Pearl Harbor, Lieutenant Robert Anderson issued a call for "more women" volunteers as he expanded operations at the filter center. Realizing that all able-bodied men within service age needed to report for military induction, Anderson wanted to add to the 150 individuals already helping at the filter center. Each woman remained at her telephone booth for six hours; rotating shifts allowed for twenty-seven women to work at the center at any given moment.

Filter center volunteers received a quick course in map reading, as their main job was to plot the called-in aircraft sightings, highlighting important data such as the number of aircraft, direction flying and estimated altitude. Tellers would then report the findings to the Aircraft Warning Service (AWS) regional office in the Bay Area; from there, the military notified interceptor planes. Pacific Gas & Electric installed a direct telephone line

North State spotters used binoculars when available and communicated any sightings by telephoning the nearest filter center. This photo here is of an East Coast spotter. *Library of Congress.*

to the San Francisco headquarters of the AWS. To protect electric and telephone infrastructure, the company sent armed employees to all "its power development" with expressed orders to "report anything unusual."

Some counties found it difficult to recruit enough spotters. In Red Bluff, calls went out on December 8 for volunteers, but the county failed to reach anywhere near its quota of 250 spotters. Jack Armstrong, chair of the Tehama County Volunteer Service Committee, made several renewed efforts, reminding women and students in high school, boys and girls, that aircraft spotting helped the war effort in providing a first line of defense against Japanese air attack in the North State. On the contrary, the small town of Corning, to the south of Red Bluff, recruited 230 persons in less than two days. With only 75 volunteers, the Red Bluff committee called for a public meeting to talk about the issue, and according to the *Red Bluff News*, the meeting was "attended by a handful." Much of the chagrin shown by the county search committee in the Red Bluff case was over the idea that more volunteers would allow for shorter hours at observation stations, but other personal demands made it difficult for many to volunteer. Other towns in the North State also found it difficult to meet self-imposed quotas during the first few days after Pearl Harbor—confusion reigned, and many federal agencies fought for military and civilian recruits from the general population. However, in Tehama County, two local Native American tribal organizations, the Improved Order of Red Men and the Idaka Council of the Degree of Pocahontas, volunteered to serve. Both groups offered to help in whatever capacity county officials needed.

PREPARING FOR THE DEFENSE OF THE HOMELAND

Changes were taking place throughout all North State counties as the days moved on from December 7, 1941. Each county organized a "defense council" charged with the responsibility of organizing county resources to support the emerging war effort. In Shasta County, Ed Steinhauer led the way in naming ten citizens and a secretary to serve on the council. Usually, a local sheriff and attorney served on these councils; well-known attorney Laurence W. Carr and Sheriff W.W. Sublett served on the Shasta defense council. In Red Bluff, city representatives journeyed to Oroville for a Sacramento Valley division of the state league of cities, where officials wanted to share ideas for conducting air raid drills. Yreka representatives shared their plans, already in existence, and at the meetings, representatives heard remarks from Richard Graves, executive director of the State Defense Council.

It seemed as if overnight, everyone—every citizen, male or female, child or adult—needed to answer a call for the defense of the homeland. Local newspapers spread the word. The *Redding Record* made its patriotic pitch:

> *In the days to come this individual pledge of support is going to be more than a phrase. You may find yourself asked to volunteer for duty in the state guard, in the aircraft warning service, in Red Cross work, in nursing, in civilian defense, or some other activity. Certainly, you will be called upon to buy defense stamps and bonds, and both directly and indirectly you will help through the payment of taxes.... To us, in Shasta County, the war with Japan is something real and immediate. We are only 150 miles from the shore of the Pacific, and no one knows what parts of that ocean may come into action. A full-scale invasion of the Pacific coast seems inconceivable now, but the landing of raiding parties and the sending of bombing planes is quite possible. With vital roads and vital power plants in our vicinity, we may see enemy action or sabotage....One thing we can all do to help is to "keep our shirts on." We must not get hysterical. We must not spread unconfirmed and alarming rumors. We must remember that military vehicles and military needs now have the right of way.*[2]

Officials at Pacific Gas and Electric regarded the Japanese threat seriously; they planned for additional security at key installations and immediately "speeded its construction program to provide additional power resources to meet the constantly mounting demand."[3] Workers completed new power plants on the Yuba River in Nevada County (1942) and Bear River in Placer County (1943); however, two proposed hydro plants for the Feather River did not receive proper licenses and were abandoned. In Shasta County, Pit 5 Powerhouse at Big Bend became a priority with work started before Pearl Harbor. A twenty-four-hour work schedule pressed forward in an effort to finish the plant, employing over one thousand men to build a diversion dam. With the North State as the best source of hydroelectric power, PG&E worked consistently and successfully with the Bureau of Reclamation, state water officials and local communities to ensure generating capacity remained at the highest level. Pressure continued as war-related manufacturing plants sprouted throughout the state, including shipyards, aluminum and magnesium plants and a wide assortment of military-related auxiliary businesses.

Much of the fear spreading across the North State and all of California arose from the perceived threat of an imminent air attack by Japanese planes launched from an offshore aircraft carrier. The first air raid sirens blasted off and on for days as false reports poured into the AWS center in San Francisco. Most of the reporting incorrectly identified navy patrol bombers returning to bases around the Bay Area. In the North State counties, defense councils working with military officials organized their own air raid warning program. Redding mayor August Gronwoldt organized local shop owners and other citizens to prepare for a blackout of all buildings should AWS observers spot enemy planes over the coastal city of Eureka, a distance of only one hundred air miles away. Officials decided to use the fire station warning horn: short bursts for a period of two minutes, followed by one long blast announcing the all clear. At the same time, Shasta Dam workers living in the newly formed communities in Central Valley and Project City agreed to use an identical signal pattern. Instructions for these communities quickly followed, requiring all persons at home or working in commercial buildings to turn off all electrical lights and motorists to stop their vehicles and shut off their lights.

Oroville residents read, day after day, reminders of the correct procedures they were required to follow when the air raid signal blared. These included:

Put out all lights including auto headlights.
Drive to the right-hand curb avoiding fireplugs; keep the key in car.
Don't hurry, remain calm. Better to drive two blocks than to double-park.
Do not use the telephone.
Stay at home, if bombs begin to fall, lie flat against an interior wall.
Prepare buckets of dry sand to smother incendiary bombs; never turn a stream of water direct upon such a bomb but use a very fine spray.
Clear your attic of incendiary materials—officials recommended placing a two-inch layer of sand on the attic floor.[4]

Jittery Oroville families, at first, reacted to the sound of every airplane sighted overhead, but when lights flashed on or near the planes, the phone lines rang out in response. This scenario happened when three newly assigned friendly aircraft were cruising one cloudless night in early January 1942. The pilots' practicing their nighttime signal communications with bright signal lights was misinterpreted by some as the precursor to dropping sighting flares, in itself a precursor to dropping a nighttime load of bombs; such was the high state of anxiety weeks after Pearl Harbor. Apprehension heightened when local citizens saw some residents walking around town wearing old World War I gas masks. Local law enforcement officials immediately printed

Apparently, several North State residents appeared in public wearing World War I gas masks, to the chagrin of officials, who quickly learned from military sources that the masks might no longer provide sufficient protection. An American soldier from that previous conflict is shown above, with his gas mask hanging in front. *Library of Congress.*

a warning stating the masks "are no longer effective." Apparently, a run on the purchase of these old masks pervaded much of the country in the early months of the war, despite authorities' warning of possible malfunctions.

Tehama County sheriff James Froome, charged with the responsibility of organizing blackout rules and procedures for his county, expected several rehearsed opportunities by the military to stage a few practice blackout drills, but to his chagrin, he found out otherwise. Local news outlets reported that "army officials said that orders for blackout would come direct from interceptor command headquarters [San Francisco] and there would be no practice." However, Froome contacted Red Bluff and Corning officials and began preparing a coordinated effort for uniform blackout rules and procedures.[5]

Meanwhile, at the Shasta Dam construction site, the Bureau of Reclamation placed armed guards on duty at key locations. This included Keswick Dam, along the miles-long conveyor belt from Redding, and at the Pitt River Bridge; officials decided all locations needed guarding around the clock. The bureau working with local sheriffs allowed newly sworn-in deputies to help in this effort; it seemed as if everyone carried a gun, usually a rifle. Southern Pacific Railroad officials, worried about their tracks and stations, asked for and received help from army units in the Bay Area. Dozens of soldiers arrived in each county, patrolling station warehouses and key railroad bridges, guns loaded and ready to check access papers.

As younger men, eighteen to thirty-five years of age, pondered enlisting in the army, navy or Army Air Corps, older men signed on to serve in local units of the California State Guard. In Redding, new recruits mustered in, bringing that unit to 108 individuals, a full company. Practice drilling began at Shasta Union High School, with expectations by local government officials for patrolling downtown areas and county areas deemed potential targets, as determined by army officials in Sacramento. The formal swearing-in ceremony, held at the Veteran's Memorial Hall, brought a large crowd of family members and interested local citizens. In Red Bluff, a large advertisement appeared in the *Daily News* for days after the Pearl Harbor attack, declaring that "All Men Who Wish to Do Their Part" should enlist now in the state guard. A hastily organized meeting held at the local armory included veterans and current guard members; current guard members attended to explain enlistment procedures and answer questions. Proudly known as the "behind-the-scenes-Army," the state guard grew in size as the war dragged on during 1942. Guardsmen's responsibilities included guarding harbor installations and shipyards in the Bay Area and steel

Above: With the designated priority defense rating, the War Department ordered a detachment of soldiers for guard duty as needed by the Bureau of Reclamation. The soldier shown above is guarding the railroad tunnel at the dam site immediately after the Pearl Harbor attack. *Bureau of Reclamation.*

Opposite: All through the war, local North State families tried their best to honor their traditional holiday festivities, attending family and community-sponsored events. Local stores, such as Bradley's in Marysville, continued to run gift ads up until Christmas during the weeks after Pearl Harbor. *From the* Gridley Herald, *December 9, 1941.*

mills and aircraft construction plants in Southern California and securing laboratories carrying on vital war weapons research—such as the California Institute of Technology in Pasadena, where defense equipment underwent experimental testing.

The interesting background of the California State Guard saw it drawing North State residents between the ages of eighteen to sixty. They resumed the duties formerly undertaken by the National Guard. The National Guard was now quickly called up to active duty in the military. North State residents soon understood that the state guard existed as a cooperating unit between army and navy commands and local civilian authorities, including city police and county sheriffs. Their responsibilities expanded during this time to protecting not only "California's property" but also, now, the fast-growing defense industries against foreign and domestic sabotage or in direct invasion scenarios. Interestingly, at the beginning of the war, with a huge Japanese invasion expected, the possibility arose of—and plans were made for—calling the state guard to act independently as "guerrilla" units, "if that should seem feasible."[6]

During the final weeks of 1941, a massive rush for a call to arms arose, asking everyone to become involved as a formal duty of Californians and American citizens despite the approaching traditional Christmas celebration period. Desiring to do its part, the Shasta County Grand Jury assembled in a special session and announced its support in helping coordinate defense plans and programs, reminding everyone of their solemn duty. The grand jury declared in a formal statement, "We pledge our loyal and unified support to all coordinating bodies, and we ask and request everyone in Redding and Shasta County to unite in this, the time of defense of home and country."[7]

With sabotage on everyone's mind, travel restrictions soon appeared. Columbia Construction Company, responsible for building and maintaining the miles-long conveyor belt that continually delivered gravel of various sizes to the concrete-mixing site near Shasta Dam, previously used as a quick transportation route between Redding and the boomtowns growing around Central Valley, made a decision to shut down road access. This road closed just days after Pearl Harbor; the company even restricted employees from driving their own automobiles, declaring that only company-supplied vehicles may use the route until further notice, citing sabotage as the reason.

ENLISTING FOR THE MILITARY

Shasta County served as a regional far-northern California enlistment center. By the end of December 1941, men from surrounding mountain communities were making their way to Redding. There they volunteered to serve, presenting themselves at either the army or navy enlistment headquarters. Far northeastern Modoc County saw twelve men drive a long distance to enlist in the navy, all in one day. From Weaverville in Trinity County to Lassen County in the east, more men reported for duty. The Redding enlistment centers stretched their operating hours, remaining open on certain days to eleven o'clock at night. The North State was answering the call to duty.

Speaking of the U.S. Navy, it quickly began vying with army advertisements to draw young men and women to its service. One navy ad listed all the benefits of a navy career:

> *Free training: worth $1,500, all trades and vocations to choose from.*
> *Good Pay: with regular increments. You may earn up to $135 a month.*
> *Each Year: you are entitled to a generous vacation period with full pay.*
> *Good Food: and plenty of it.*

Free Clothing: A complete outfit of clothing when you first enlist, worth over $100.

Free Medical Care: also regular dental care.

Finest Sports: and entertainment.

Travel, Adventure, Thrills: You can't beat this Navy for them!

Become an Officer: Many can work for an appointment to the Naval Academy or the Annapolis of the Air.

Future Success: It's usual for Navy-trained men to get good-paying jobs in civilian life.

Liberal Retirement: Pay for regular Navy men.[8]

The ads listed the respectable trades offered to navy recruits; readers found priority given to training men for jobs as "mechanics, electricians, radiomen, signalmen, carpenters, and other specialties": a choice of over forty-five occupations existed for new recruits. Of course, the army could offer many of the same opportunities, but the navy kept reminding young men and women that in the navy, they could have adventures abroad visiting exciting seaports in the Atlantic and Pacific while protecting the shorelines of America. On another interesting front, the navy talked about helping young men and women achieve "their own security and independence," two personal goals many young people growing up in the Great Depression desired.

During the last weeks of 1941, much discussion arose over the issue of conscientious objectors. Without referencing specific individuals, articles appeared in local newspapers arguing the pros and cons of those young men declaring a "higher calling" to personal actions. On the one hand, most writers saw the need for all citizens to answer the call for military action in whatever capacity the government deemed necessary. Others raised the concern as a religious issue that Americans traditionally honored in cases where evidence revealed a sincerity of belief. One article noted, "A Christian should serve the state in all ways which are compatible with his [and her] obligation to God,"[9] refusing any duty or service contrary to personal beliefs. On another issue, a seventeen-year-old boy in Siskiyou County received a school suspension for refusing to salute the flag. The boy, whose family followed the tenets of the Jehovah's Witnesses religion, sat quietly as the high school principal told the student body that President Roosevelt was about to address the nation with a declaration of war against Japan.

Consternation remained visible throughout the North State, with conflicting messages from local, state and federal agencies and authorities. For example, everyone wanted to abide by the new blackout rules, but

Navy recruitment advertisements began to appear in large numbers as 1942 opened. As seen from the listed inducements noted earlier, many young men from the North State chose the navy. *National Archives.*

many questions remained unanswered. To end the confusion, local officials contacted army headquarters in San Francisco for help in delineating the particulars of blackout rules and tips. By the beginning of 1942, local political and law enforcement leaders had distributed sets of blackout regulations to all citizens. Everyone was to have at least one "blackout room," to which all members of the household would go in times of air raid alert. Officials encouraged people to make this room the kitchen, since it was necessary to have access to food and water. In this blackout room, the rules suggested a light may be kept on as long as no light escaped to the outside. Homeowners, under direct orders, were to go outside and examine all windows and doors. Of particular importance for homes without roof overhangs was the concern for light escaping at the top of windows, thereby making it visible from the sky above; homeowners needed to check this possibility carefully. Going further, one article noted, "Persons also should determine whether light is escaping from under doors or other cracks in the room." Redding police chief John Balma stressed the importance of ensuring homes did a "complete blackout," citing military references stating that a single lighted match could be seen from an altitude of four thousand feet. W.J. Clarke, manager of the Pacific Telephone and Telegraph, reminded residents not to make phone calls during blackouts except in case of emergency.

North State residents, expecting a war with Germany, woke to the news a few days after Pearl Harbor to find their expectations proved true. Germany and fellow Axis partner Italy had declared war. Now, early optimism for a short, one-ocean war dissipated as rumors spread of a two-ocean war involving a massive commitment of military personnel, logistical support and ongoing home front involvement. Immediately, local police departments and civilian defense organizations in every North State county asked, and then demanded, that anyone who had not volunteered up to that point needed to step forward now. The realization struck home, as one person commented, "Now, it's a real global war. There will be fighting everywhere." He was right.

NORTH STATE RESIDENTS IN THE PACIFIC DURING THE PEARL HARBOR ATTACK

Along with the ominous news of an expanded war involvement, at least two North State families received good news. The army and the federal government, by December 12, 1941, had begun to notify North State families of their sons' combat status. Mrs. Edith Woodrum exploded in celebration after opening the cablegram that confirmed her son, Henry, had survived the Pearl Harbor attack unharmed. Two boys, Carroll and Dwight, also were able to get a cablegram through to their parents. Dwight, in the marine corps, saw action on December 7, but he was not injured. Carroll noted that he and his wife, though scared during the attack, remained safe throughout the fighting.

Sadly, Richard Minear of Redding learned by cablegram from the War Department that his son Richard Jr. died in combat on the battleship USS *Arizona*, sunk by Japanese bombs and torpedoes. Serving as a marine on the famed fighting ship, Minear became one of the first gold star recipients to appear on Redding's service flag. In Tehama County, the first combat death came to Keith Milbourne, only twenty-one years old at the time. The Navy Department issued the statement to his parents, who were then residing in Corning; the military provided no details.

Early in January, one North State civilian, Marcia Whitlock, returned by ship from Honolulu. Whitlock, a resident of Oroville, witnessed the attack on Pearl Harbor while working in a nearby construction company. When questioned about the situation in Hawaii, she said, "People seem to be more nervous in San Francisco than they are in Honolulu." The happy returning resident noted that her ship was part of a three-ship convoy of returning civilians, wounded American soldiers and sailors and the families of "army and navy men."[10] She went on to describe the continual zigzag tracks that all three ships maintained for fear of a Japanese submarine attack. Lamenting that the ship's captain refused to run the onboard water-condensing machine, fearing the noise might reveal the vessel's position, Whitlock recalled that passengers responded by singing, "I am a refugee from Waikiki, and I haven't had a bath." Her experience on December 7 reflected a combination of fear and curiosity. Asleep when the first bombs dropped, young Whitlock turned on the radio, listened for a short time, then decided to watch the fighting from a nearby fort, counting twenty enemy planes flying high and diving quickly downward for a strike and observing smoke from battleship row rising high into the sky. Her uncle, Robert Ely, a onetime Oroville resident also on Oahu, heard nothing at first as he began a round of golf.[11]

Following the German declaration of war, draft boards throughout the North State picked up the urgency of ensuring that all qualified candidates reported for their physical examinations, a required prerequisite for joining the military. In fact, one county, Shasta, decided to publicize the names of any individuals failing to show on their given date of examination. Some

The USS *Arizona* received many hits from Japanese bombs; one bomb that hit in the front of the battleship penetrated the deck and exploded where much of the ammunition for the main guns were stored. As a result, the battleship sustained major destruction, as can be seen in the photo above. Over 1,100 men died onboard or in the waters immediately surrounding the ship. *Library of Congress.*

notations included home addresses or places of work—a hint that someone might visit shortly to remind them of their duty. While all this was going on, Redding building inspectors reported publicly that only three buildings— the county jail, the city fire hall and the Pacific Telephone & Telegraph building—"could withstand direct hits with projectiles of any size." These buildings, constructed with reinforced concrete, remained among the few in the entire North State capable of offering some protection from air attack.

Chapter 2

JAPANESE AMERICAN INTERNMENT

Marysville Assembly Center

CONCERN OVER NORTH STATE PERSONS
OF JAPANESE DESCENT

Throughout the state, agents of the Federal Bureau of Investigation (FBI) scoured each county for suspect Japanese "nationals." While the bureau never gave a clear reason for subsequent arrests, each person was booked under "open charges for investigation" or as "en route to the U.S. immigration bureau." The bureau admitted that most of the persons arrested held jobs in business or worked professionally occupied as merchants, physicians "and the like." Along with handcuffing these Japanese "aliens," the FBI seized "papers and other possessions belonging to the Japanese." This same article appearing in the *Daily News* on December 8, 1941, reported that the director of the state finance office, George Kittlon, called federal authorities to offer "12 relief camps…for use as internment centers for alien Japanese."

War hysteria, brought on by the sudden attack at Pearl Harbor, immediately drew condemnation and suspicion of anyone of Japanese descent. As early as September 1941, military officials were sent to Hawaii to discuss plans to "intern enemy aliens" if war should come. After the attack, government officials placed the Hawaiian Islands, which at that time counted a large ethnic Japanese population, under martial law. Now, questions arose about the approximately 112,000 Japanese Americans living along the West Coast. Regionally, North State officials waited to hear from federal and state agencies and the military concerning local citizens of Japanese descent. However, at the municipal level, one of the first to provide guidance was Chico chief of police C.E. Tovee. On December 8, 1941, Red Bluff residents read in their local newspaper a stern notice from Tovee. Worried about the connection between the overconsumption of liquor and war anxiety toward "foreign nationals," he wrote,

> The time has come for every community in America to be sober and industrious—I refer primarily to the sale of alcoholic liquors. The cooperation of all liquor dealers is necessary at this time as an aid in the defense of Chico and the entire country....A number of precautionary measures have been taken. We are ready for any emergency. I have conferred by telephone with the San Francisco office of the Federal Bureau of Investigation, and I was notified to do everything possible to prevent hysteria. There is no cause for alarm here, and the citizens are urged to go about their regular business as usual. Foreign nationals, as long as they cause no trouble, should be given every consideration, and they will certainly be given police protection. We must remember that there are many American nationals in Japan and any outbreaks here might lead to reprisals.

The promise of police protection may or may not have eased the concerns of Japanese American residents, but they remained worried about their children. For a number of days following the attack on Pearl Harbor, Butte County school officials reported "many" students of Japanese heritage not attending their classes. A notice from Tovee declaring there was "no reason" for Japanese American students to remain home did not help resolve the situation. At school, teachers in the upper grades allowed students to listen to radio broadcasts from President Franklin D. Roosevelt, other politicians and military leaders. Recalling the buildup to World War II, Chico school superintendent F.F. Martin noted, "For two years Chico's school teachers and officials have been coached to handle just such a war emergency." Despite the proactive training of teachers to handle a wartime demographic situation, the social situation in the North State, as everywhere throughout California and the nation, remained confused, even tense, with anxiety building every day.

A nationwide storm of anger over the surprise attack on Pearl Harbor put immediate pressure on the military and the president to consider what do to with "enemy aliens" living within the national boundaries of American territories and states. President Franklin Roosevelt, on the

C. E. Order 47

WESTERN DEFENSE COMMAND AND FOURTH ARMY
WARTIME CIVIL CONTROL ADMINISTRATION
Presidio of San Francisco, California

INSTRUCTIONS

TO ALL PERSONS OF

JAPANESE

ANCESTRY

LIVING IN THE FOLLOWING AREA:

All that portion of the County of Placer, State of California, within the boundary beginning at a point at which U. S. Highway No. 99E intersects the Placer-Yuba County line, at or near Wheatland; thence southeasterly and following said Highway No. 99E to its intersection with a paved road running easterly from Lincoln to Newcastle; thence easterly and following said improved road to the point at which it intersects U. S. Highway No. 40, at or near Newcastle; thence southwesterly and following said Highway No. 40 to Loomis; thence southerly on an improved road running from Loomis to Folsom, to the Placer-Sacramento County line; thence westerly along said county line to Sutter-Placer County line; thence northerly along said county line to the point of beginning.

Pursuant to the provisions of Civilian Exclusion Order No. 47, this Headquarters, dated May 7, 1942, all persons of Japanese ancestry, both alien and non-alien, will be evacuated from the above area by 12 o'clock noon, P.W.T., Thursday, May 14, 1942.

No Japanese person living in the above area will be permitted to change residence after 12 o'clock noon, P.W.T., Thursday, May 7, 1942, without obtaining special permission from the representative of the Commanding General, Northern California Sector, at the Civil Control Station located at:

Loomis Union Grammar School,
Loomis, California.

This local notice gave instructions to persons of Japanese descent living in Placer County, including the towns of Wheatland, Lincoln, Newcastle, Loomis and Folsom and taking in all areas within the boundaries defined above by Highways 99 and 40. *National Archives and Records Administration.*

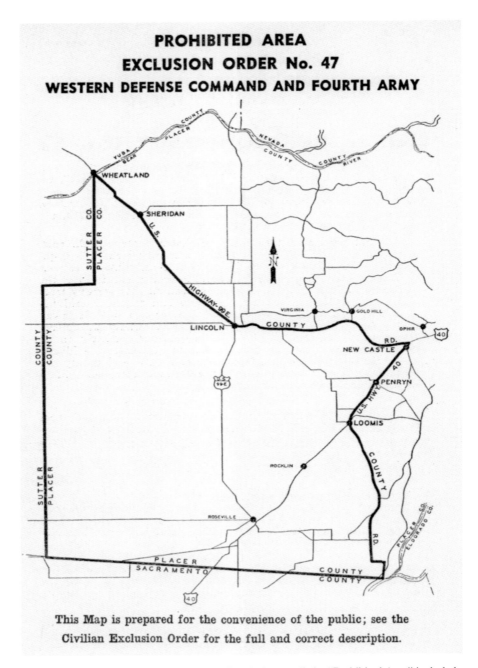

This Map is prepared for the convenience of the public; see the Civilian Exclusion Order for the full and correct description.

What the Western Defense Command and Fourth Army called a "Prohibited Area" included most of the Japanese Americans living in the region. Other exclusion orders covered different counties, including Sutter and Sacramento. *National Archives and Records Administration.*

afternoon of the attack, authorized the military to work in concert with the FBI to identify enemy aliens, Japanese, Italian and German, that might pose a danger to the nation and its military response. General John DeWitt, the military commander at the Western Defense Command at the Presidio of San Francisco, declared as early as December 19, 1941, his initial position on the subject. He at first demurred over the idea of rounding up more than one hundred thousand West Coast residents of Japanese ancestry. As the weeks went on and the full disclosure of the death and destruction at Pearl Harbor reached deeper into the American psyche, public pressure mounted for the removal of both Issei, first-generation Japanese Americans, and Nisei, natural-born residents. Finally, by the end of January, De Witt, after receiving numerous unconfirmed reports of suspicious radio transmissions from up and down the West Coast, especially California, recommended the exclusion of enemy aliens from various key areas near military bases.[12]

THE MARYSVILLE ASSEMBLY CENTER (ARBOGA)

By February, Roosevelt agreed to the evacuation request, issuing Executive Order 9066, which allowed military leaders to begin planning the removal of all Japanese Americans on the West Coast. Meanwhile, newspapers reported public reaction, including acts of violence from vigilantes toward Japanese Americans living in Los Angeles and other cities—additional motivation to act quickly. The military decided to set up temporary assembly or detention centers to facilitate the urgent task of relocation. The next month, March, saw the beginning of construction for the Marysville Assembly Center (Arboga), located eight miles south of the town of Marysville. Situated on a level area formerly used as a migrant labor camp, the Marysville Assembly Center contained over one hundred buildings, laid out in rectangular rows, consisting of housing huts, large dining rooms and a medical building.

Interestingly, the very hour President Roosevelt stood before Congress to declare war on Japan, the leadership of the Japanese American Citizens' League (JACL) presented a resolution to Marysville mayor Charles Hust, "reaffirming 'without any reservation' its allegiance to the United States." Frank Nakamura, president of the JACL, promised that its members would "report and resist un-American actions from whatever source they may be found." He went on to pledge to "cooperate with other local organizations in whatever manner we find possible." In a final resolution, the organization desired to declare its allegiance publicly: "Before our governing bodies, public officials, and fellow American citizens we state as follows: We, American citizens of Japanese ancestry, by unanimous thought and action, are loyal citizens of the United States."[13]

In a separate article on December 8, Frank Nakamura reminded readers that twenty-five Japanese Americans, residents of the Marysville–Yuba City area, were currently serving in the military. Right after Roosevelt concluded his war declaration speech, Nakamura told a reporter, "I am just past 28 [years old] and was married last month, being deferred in the draft because of my age. Now I expect to be called and will serve gladly. I feel that my family will be treated fairly while I am gone." In the same interview, Mrs. C. Coda, a Japanese-language teacher, wanted to make a statement; "I know that American-born Japanese are good American citizens. You can expect the people will treat you as citizens and work together for an early peace."[14]

Whatever local citizens may have felt about their Japanese American neighbors, the president and the military moved forward with evacuation

The camp consisted of an administration building, 126 barracks, 7 mess halls, 15 warehouses, guard towers, latrines, laundry areas and a couple of small hospitals. The Marysville camp served as a temporary holding facility until the much larger camp in Tule Lake became available. *California Military Museum.*

Arboga Assembly Center

This is the site of Arboga, where 2,465 Japanese Americans forced from their homes in Placer and Sacramento Counties were incarcerated from May 8 to June 29, 1942, by the United States Government. Four months prior, on February 19, 1942, President Franklin Delano Roosevelt signed Executive Order 9066, which unjustifiable ordered the removal of all persons of Japanese ancestry from the West Coast. Henceforth, may constitutional rights be unquestionably upheld in these United States of America

Dedicated on February 27, 2010

Sponsors include: California State Parks, Marysville Joint Unified School District, Yuba County Board of Supervisors, Friends for the Preservation of Yuba County History, National Park Service, Marysville Buddhist Church, Marysville Chapter Japanese American Citizens League and others.

California State Historical Landmark No. 934

The above graphic is a replica of the plaque that now stands at the former Marysville Assembly Center (Arboga); the land is currently privately owned. *Author's collection.*

plans. By May, the completed camp stood ready to receive its first group of Japanese Americans, coming mainly from the Roseville, Rocklin and Loomis areas. A second large group came later that month from Florin, Elk Grove and other rural areas in the Sacramento area. By the end of May, over two thousand Japanese Americans resided in the temporary camp, awaiting a decision by the military as to their final destination.

The 160-acre converted camp left much to be desired, as residents struggled to adjust to a restricted, confined living environment. Although local and military inspectors approved the site as ready for habitation, everything seemed to go wrong from the beginning. Late rains allowed for an unusually high number of mosquitos to breed in and around the camp, entering barracks through every conceivable physical opportunity—even the floorboards, separated now with the late spring heat, allowed untold hordes of the annoying insects to cause havoc, especially with the children. One group of residents tried, with limited success, to place screen netting on the floor. Another concerned person recalled the mosquitos being so numerous that they covered every light bulb in the building. The sinks did not supply hot water, and the bathroom facilities consisted of makeshift pits, separate pits for men and women yet without privacy dividers between the cutout holes in the rough wood floor.

Many of the administrative staff from local Works Progress Administration (WPA) offices ran the day-to-day affairs of the Marysville Assembly Center. Paul D. Shriver arrived to initiate the camp opening; Nicholas L. Bican, who stayed until the camp shut down in June, followed him. These administrators attempted to bring some semblance of normalcy to camp life, realizing that this particular camp served only as a holding site until permanent facilities were completed somewhere else in the state or nation. From early on, Shriver and Bican allowed each block of barracks to elect monitors to serve as representatives of the people, with the ability to report problems or concerns.

Late in May, a small library opened that made available magazines and a few books loaned from local North State libraries. An attempt to start a small newspaper moved forward, with complaints from many Japanese Americans who wanted to write about conditions in the camp but incurred regular censorship of "controversial topics."[15] A resolution for honoring residents who wanted a place of worship included the conversion of one barracks-type building, allowing a large number of Buddhists and a small number of Christians, Protestant and Catholic, a place for church activities. For recreation, weekly dances, arts and crafts classes or clubs and a glee club offered some relief from the boredom of everyday camp life.

The local Marysville newspaper, the *Appeal-Democrat*, on the same week that the assembly camp opened, let readers know that in the Portland area, where an assembly camp was already operating, that the "Japanese apparently have little complaint against their confinement." This observation was made based on evidence that a few Japanese in the Portland camp volunteered to work under minimum supervision harvesting beets in the eastern portion of the state or nearby Idaho. Later, in June, nine evacuees in the Marysville camp volunteered to go to Idaho, but "red tape" held up the process. In describing the Marysville campsite, the paper noted, "In the camps, they are living comfortably, with food that they like, provision for recreation, an organized health service, and an active work program (paid in wages)."[16] The article insisted that ample freedom within the camp existed and the

The Marysville camp did have a small store where evacuees could purchase some food and dry goods; this photo from the Pomona Assembly Center shows newly ordered apparel arriving for distribution at the camp. *Library of Congress.*

work offered to the camp families matched "well" to what existed before confinement, adding "probably are living better than they ever have before."

Local Marysville residents watched as busload after busload of new camp arrivals arrived in late May from Placer County. Interestingly, as these events occurred, military officials put the finishing touches on plans to evacuate Japanese Americans from Yuba, Sutter and Colusa Counties, all within the Defense Military Area No. 1, not to the Marysville site but some other locations more distant. Yuba City's state armory building housed a makeshift assembly area for these persons, registering families as they reported.

Meanwhile, in the Marysville Assembly Center, administrators from Washington State and San Francisco arrived to ensure efficient camp operations. W.A. Dougherty, assistant camp director, completed an initial camp inspection; he noted that the post office and canteen, now completed, offered residents opportunities to communicate outside the confines of the assembly center with "no censorship beyond an inspection of packages."

The canteen accepted payment of personal goods with "a script purchased from the center cashier." Due to the temporary nature of the assembly center, the government, from the beginning, did not plan for educational programs. However, a newspaper article remarked that since the evacuation occurred toward the end of the school year, it would be possible to award diplomas to graduating eighth-grade and high school students. Yet this was not to be. On June 4, 1942, confusion reigned for days among local school authorities, regional officials and army headquarters in San Francisco over the graduation issue. General DeWitt's original orders for Military Area no. 2 (North State) gave permission for Japanese American high school and college graduates to attend final ceremonies, and that had been the understanding when the camp opened. However, at the last minute, one local official decided to obtain verification to that effect, contacting the San Francisco military office; the answer was quick, "and it was decidedly negative."

CAMP RESIDENTS REMEMBER

Sometime later, Marysville Assembly Center resident Tamotsu Shibutani recalled his experiences living and working at the facility.

The food was lousy....It was hot as hell in there [the mess hall] *in May and June. We were in camp for about five weeks which were in the hottest period. Gnats were flying all over the place....No one knew what to cook....I don't think anyone enjoyed the mess food. Quite a few never ate in the mess hall. They just had their friends bring them stuff on visitors' day. Everyone devised methods to get edibles from the outside. They confidentially had the* [local] *bakery man unload several hundred dollars of bakery privately. Others had Caucasian workers purchase staple foods from the outside and sometimes paid twice and three times the actual cost.*[17]

By June 28, 1942, the last of the Japanese American camp residents had left for other more permanent facilities, and most residents were forcibly transferred to Tule Lake in northeastern California. Shibutani recalled his last days in camp:

We all knew we were leaving about one [p.m.], *but it was so damn hot we all stretched out in the shade of the barracks and just sat around. We*

The photo above was taken at the Pomona, California assembly center and is typical of the kind of kitchen facilities built and run in various temporary assembly centers during the early part of World War II. *Library of Congress.*

just gabbed and waited for lunch. The place was lonely, quiet, and deserted. The guard towers were empty. There were a few soldiers walking around in the soldiers' area. About 1:30 in the afternoon, we left Arboga [the camp]. As we drove through the gate there were no goodbyes and nobody saying, "We'll see you soon." We were the last ones to leave and all of us were happy to get out of there. A few of the people had regrets. Not about Arboga itself but because they were going farther away from home [Tule Lake]. The majority were happy to leave the cramped quarters of the concentration camp. It was a relief like being released from a civilian jail. We all felt that as we rode along the highway toward the railroad station.[18]

The property in Marysville eventually deteriorated and returned to private ownership. In 1980, California recognized the site as a California Historical Landmark (No. 394). One Japanese resident in Butte County did not move out with the other incarcerated families. Tanakichi Nakamoto, stricken

This photo of the Pomona Assembly Center shows evacuees moving through the outer gate of the camp and walking down the road to pick up buses that will take them to their main relocation camp, a scene typical of the Marysville Center experience. *Library of Congress.*

with an undisclosed illness, possibly tuberculosis, remained isolated in the Butte County hospital for over a year, then suddenly died. An American resident for over forty-five years, Nakamoto lived in California for fourteen years before the war began. Living south of Gridley, the rest of his family, his wife and others eventually were forced from the area to the Granada Resettlement Project in Granada, Colorado. The family was notified in early 1943; his son had already joined the army, receiving the news of his father's death at his station in Camp Savage, Minnesota.[19]

Those Japanese Americans sent to Tule Lake witnessed a homicide in the middle of 1944. The victim, Shiochi James Okomoto, an American-born Japanese, was shot and killed by a military sentry at the Tule Lake segregation center, camp director Ray R. Best announced on May 27.[20] According to one account, Okomoto retained his responsibility of driving a truck from the camp to a "worksite" located some distance away; presumably he performed this duty regularly. However, on May 24, 1944, when he returned to the camp entrance, stopped and waited for the sentry to flag him through, the armed guard asked Okomoto to get out of the truck and show his official authorization pass instead. The Japanese American stepped down from his vehicle, but he would not show the pass, whereupon the sentry raised his rifle and hit Okomoto on the upper chest or shoulder area. Both men, now upset, began complaining, Okomoto protesting being hit and the sentry demanding to see the pass. At this point, for some reason, the sentry raised his rifle again, this time shooting Okomoto. Immediately, guards rushed Okomoto to the camp hospital, but he died the next day; the Japanese American was only thirty years old. An investigation led to a court-martial hearing ending in the acquittal of the sentry. The soldier "was fined one dollar for the cost of the bullet fired in an 'unauthorized use of government property.'"[21] The Japanese government found out about the shooting and launched a strong protest against what they called an "overt act against humanity." Tokyo relayed the message to public radio stations for distribution around America, and the story was broadcast by NBC News.[22]

The military, later in the war, gave incarcerated Japanese Americans the option to enlist in a planned all-Nisei combat unit. Over one thousand young men did volunteer, with fifty-seven of them coming from Tule Lake; it is not known how many of these soldiers came from North State counties.[23] The 442nd Regimental Combat Team completed distinguished service in Europe, particularly in Italy and France, winning numerous awards, including a Congressional Medal of Honor and the French Légion d'honneur.

Chapter 3

ARMY/NAVY AIRFIELDS AND BASES

The United States Army Air Force (USAAF) gave responsibility for the air defense of America's West Coast to the Fourth Air Force, consisting of two major air wings in California, one in the Los Angeles area and the other in the Bay Area. By September 1941, army air officials had decided to add additional airfields for training new pilots to serve in possible combat roles. To this end, military engineers built a series of supplemental and/or emergency landing fields throughout the North State.

Chico Army Airfields

Before the war began, anticipating the need to train pilots for military service, the federal government began planning for an expansion of airfields across the country. With limited available open space and level areas in the Bay Area, the army decided to select sites in the flat topography of the Sacramento Valley. To this effect, the U.S. Army Corps of Engineers (representing the War Department), in September 1941, leased over one thousand acres of land from the city of Chico, located a few miles north of the town limits. The legal arrangement ran from September 10, 1941, through June 30, 1942, with an extension to be granted if needed; the cost came to one dollar a year.

A comprehensive flight development plan came to fruition in 1942, naming the Chico Airfield as an extension of the Tenth Army Air Force

This two-engine twin-tailed P-38 Lightning fighter was originally designed to intercept enemy bombers. Training for pilots occurred at the Chico Army Airfield. The P-38 proved devastating with its four 50-caliber machine guns and a 20-mm cannon. *Wikimedia (public domain).*

Base Unit, AAF West Coast Training Center, Army Air Forces Training Command. Officials planned for five auxiliary (i.e., emergency) airfields, including Orland Auxiliary Field No. 1, Kirkwood Auxiliary Field No. 2, Vina Auxiliary Field No. 3, Campbell Auxiliary Field No. 4 and Oroville Auxiliary Field No. 5.

Later, in November 1942, the army added the Siskiyou County Airport to cover emergency landings in the far northern region of California. Construction on the Chico airfield moved along briskly, as money, men and materials flooded the area in the first four months of 1942. Access roads, hangars, administrative buildings and barracks appeared from the dormant, level, weed-filled fields. In mid-April, personnel filed into the new facilities, with the first training cadets showing up by the end of the month, coming from the South Bay Area site at Moffett Field.

The cadets, organized by squadron, trained in the new classrooms, with progressive air flight episodes in special trainer aircraft, usually BT-13 and

Comprising 323 acres, the Vina Auxiliary Field supported the training efforts of the Chico Army Air Field, especially for practicing takeoff and landing for such aircraft as the Vultee BT-13 and BT-15 training planes. The landing field consisted of a 3,000-by-3,000-foot paved landing mat. *California Military Museum.*

This airplane served as a primary and advanced training aircraft, while a later variant BT-15 also saw service in the North State. Here we see Lieutenant James Robertson flying north of Chico. The BT-13 model carries the reputation as the training plane most used by pilots in World War II. *Nopel Collection.*

This photo taken in 1942 shows soldiers working on landscaping around some of the new buildings going up at the airfield. *Merriam Library Digital Collections.*

BT-15 models. By 1943, dozens of aircraft might be seen overhead in and around the Chico area as training pilots practiced basic flying maneuvers. One observer noted, "With about 300 aircraft taking off each morning, returning at noon, taking off again after lunch until landing about five p.m., there was constant and often frenzied activity going on."[24]

The first Women's Army Corps (WACs) personnel arrived in July 1943; later, one Black WAC unit arrived. All WACs served in support roles, such as cook, baker and mess hall attendant; some served in the Motor Corps and trained as mechanics.[25]

CAMP BEALE (BEALE AIR FORCE BASE TODAY)

The United States military needed army training facilities near the Bay Area, and it worked with Marysville city officials to gain a lease of eighty-seven thousand acres southeast of the town in 1942. Through the rest of the year, the camp, Camp Beale, grew in size to house, by October, a new "all California" trained armored division, the Thirteenth. Official ceremonies occurred later in July 1943, with state and military guests watching as dignitaries christened one tank *Oroville* and another *Butte County*.[26] California governor Earl Warren presided over the ceremony, as hundreds of curious public attendees viewed a grand parade of tanks.[27] Known as the Black Cats, the unit landed in France at the beginning of 1945 and saw action in the Ruhr Pocket operation and Bavaria (Germany); at one point, while in Austria, they set up headquarters in the house where Adolf Hitler was born. The men remained in Germany until the end of June, shipping home in the middle of July and later training at Camp Cook for possible participation in the proposed invasion of Japanese homeland islands.

Interestingly, the designation "Thirteenth Armored Division" given the unit centered on the symbolism that the number 13 signified bad luck, not for the men of this unit but rather for the enemy officers and men who would face them. Reportedly, some artists for a well-known design company drew the unit's insignia: a "formidable-looking black cat, sitting jauntily under a ladder" with symbols of bad luck all around it, including an open umbrella, a broken mirror and salt spilling onto the ground. According to sources, proponents of the insignia bragged that any enemy units that engaged the Thirteenth would suffer the probability of facing bad luck in a combat fight.[28]

During the war, Beale served as one of many prisoner-of-war camps, opening to receive captured German soldiers in May 1944. Eventually, seventeen barracks, four mess halls and supporting buildings rose along the prisoner campsite. Two guard towers, barbed wire and floodlights provided the necessary security. At its peak, Beale held 1,200 prisoners. Later, smaller satellite camps sprang up around the North State, with Chico Camp holding 475 Germans; other camps were located in Napa, Davis, Arbuckle and Windsor. Camp prisoners helped in agricultural work for local farmers while under tight security. Camp Beale also served as an army induction and discharge (in 1945) center for men entering and leaving the military.

This is the shoulder sleeve insignia for the Thirteenth Armored Division. Intensive training occurred for men of this unit in preparation for combat overseas in Europe. As part of the Third Army, the division spent over two weeks in constant combat, suffering 1,176 casualties. *Wikimedia (public domain)*.

Greyhound Provides Gridley with

5 SCHEDULES DAILY

TO

SAN FRANCISCO

LEAVE GRIDLEY

2:16 a. m., 8:27 a. m., 2:15 p. m., 5:11 p. m., 6:50 p. m.

FREQUENT DAILY DEPARTURES TO ALL POINTS

4 NORTH TO REDDING AND OREGON

4 TO SAN JOAQUIN VALLEY AND LOS ANGELES

5 TO SAN JOSE AND COAST POINTS

5 TO VALLEJO

SERVICE TO ALL ~ OF AMERICA

LOW MONEY-SAVING FARES

Depot 912 Hazel St.   Phone 13

ASA SMITH, Agent

GREYHOUND

With the ongoing gas and tire shortage, North State residents often used the services of bus companies such as Greyhound, which operated lines and stops in most towns of the region. For many, it was the most-used form of transportation when going to the Bay Area; frequent departures to San Francisco and other points, north and south, allowed citizens a chance to visit relatives and friends who may have moved for war-related jobs. *From the* Gridley Herald.

Civilian residents in Yuba County helped solve Camp Beale's transportation problems by moving personnel in and out of the base, arriving and departing to the Bay Area or other North State counties. Brigadier General Oscar Abbott, the camp commander, on January 1, 1945, commended North State public officials and ordinary local citizens for helping meet the transportation needs basic to the success of the camp. Due to overseas demands, few military vehicles existed, and the public bus line, Gibson, could not keep up with the demand as thousands of military personnel and civilian workers came and went on a regular basis. The general explained how a solution came about. "Due to the initiative displayed in this community," a unique directive obtained with local county and community officials and the military base allowed, for the first time, the use of "public carriers in the transportation of military personnel." Civilians signed up to drive personnel and supplies as needed throughout the North State "in a manner so fine as to avoid a complete breakdown in the nation's transportation system."[29] Proudly, the general added, "This, then, became a national policy almost immediately, for which this community received and deserved a great deal of credit."

NAVAL AIR TRANSPORT SERVICE COMMAND (NATSC) IN RED BLUFF

Early in February 1944, surveyors quickly determined that Red Bluff was an ideal spot to locate a transfer center airport for war material soon to be flown or shipped, via Seattle, to the Pacific theater of operations. Red Bluff, with little history of fog and other inclement conditions, beat out neighboring Benton Airfield in Redding as the site selected. Preliminary work on transforming the small Red Bluff airport into a military transport center occurred over months as men and material were flown in. By May 1944, Lieutenant Marcus Messinger arrived and was given the task of readying the field as officer-in-charge. The United States Weather Bureau relocated from Redding to the Red Bluff field and officially redesignated the location as Navy Ferry Station (Ferry Service Center-9). By the end of the year, construction was nearing completion, with new buildings, planes and personnel. Eventually, the field and its operations became a model for air transfer trainees sent to other western locations. Local residents came to the field regularly to view the varied aircraft and the transfer operation.

National Guard Chico's Company G, 184th Infantry Regiment (40th Infantry Division)

During World War I, military generals requested that all national guard units be constituted into the regular army units, and in the North State, they created the 49th Division to join the massive buildup of American forces to fight in 1917. The unit became mobilized again in March 1941, before the attack on Pearl Harbor. The North State contingent of the national guard now became the 184th Infantry Division. Scores of Chico's young men enlisted and, after basic training, moved to defensive positions around San Diego, as military leaders understood the strategic value of San Diego's naval facilities and harbor. Later, they relocated to Fort Lewis, Washington, and then to the Presidio in San Francisco. With unit realignment, the 184th spent time at the extensive training center at Fort Ord in the Monterey area as part of the 7th Infantry Division and the Amphibious Training Force

This photo reveals the intense combat taking place on the Kwajalein Atoll in the Pacific, with soldiers of the 184th pinned down in front of Japanese fortifications. The engagement began on February 1, 1944, and lasted until February 3. *California Military Museum.*

Here, soldiers of the 184th Infantry Division pause for a photo with a captured Japanese artillery piece. At one point in the fighting, American units became isolated; such was the case with the 184th, for a short time. Luckily, the Japanese did not attack during this time. *California Military Museum.*

Nine. Their first assignment outside of California came in the summer of 1943 when they were sent to the Aleutian Islands, receiving special training on Adak Island focused on maintaining combat effectiveness in a cold climate, including assault tactics on small islands. Their first action came in August with a landing on Kiska Island; during an unopposed beach landing, the Chico unit, Company G, discovered no opposition inland, as the enemy had previously evacuated sometime earlier. As soldiers moved from hut to hut, they saw uneaten meals and half-filled cups remaining on tables; apparently, the Japanese had realized their position on the island looked bleak. As one source stated, "Nevertheless, Company G and the 184th did have the honor of being the only National Guard regiment to regain lost American territory from a foreign enemy in World War II."[30]

After a brief respite in Honolulu, Company G left with other units for intense fighting around the Marshall Islands. An attack planned on the heavily defended Kwajalein Atoll presented a difficult situation. The island, held by the Japanese for decades before the war started, boasted considerable concrete defensive fortifications and a significant number of determined defenders, resolved to fight to the death rather than surrender.

After five days of intense fighting, some of it savage hand-to-hand encounters, the American forces prevailed. Again, Company G gained honor, being the first National Guard unit to capture Japanese territory held before Pearl Harbor. Back in Hawaii for rest and additional training, the 184th participated in the liberation of the Philippines Islands, facing stiff resistance and suffering considerable casualties. The unit received a special commendation, the Philippine Presidential Unit Citation, for commendable service from October 17, 1944, to July 4, 1945.

While fighting in the Philippines revealed the extent to which Japanese resistance had become a harsh reality, it was slight compared to what occurred when Company G participated in the Battle of Okinawa, helping capture Kadena Airfield early in the island invasion. However, while the early going looked promising, heavily fortified Japanese positions inland proved more challenging, and some companies reported losing 30 to 50 men per day. The battle dragged on as Japanese forces dug in and refused to surrender. Finally, on June 22, 1945, victory was secured. Okinawa became the bloodiest battle of the Pacific theater of war with almost the entire Japanese force, over 100,000 men, as fatalities and only 10,755 surrendering; American losses stood at 7,613 killed and 36,000 wounded. Decimated and exhausted, Company G from Chico came home to America.

STATE MILITIA (GRIDLEY)

As soon as existing National Guard units in California received orders for induction into the regular army, Congress allowed each state to raise "State Guard" or "Home Guard" units, otherwise known during World War II as state militias. Each unit, under the auspices of the War Department, would receive training for combat and only minimal weapons; the number of militia recruits was set at half the strength of the preexisting National Guard unit from that state. Area Guard commanders issued some military-grade rifles for local distribution in early 1942, but the military called them back for use overseas, later changing that policy as the state units protested being "disarmed." The primary functions of these citizen soldiers included guarding local physical facilities deemed important to the war effort, such as small dams, electrical power plants and the power grid, hospitals, local airports and, in California's case, miles and miles of shoreline. Official declarations made it clear that membership in the state militia precluded units from "being called, drafted, or ordered into Federal service, nor could these troops be ordered to serve outside the boundaries of their own states."[31]

One example of an active state militia group during the war can be seen in the so-called Gridley Rifles. Sergeant Clarence Bassett, in charge of public relations for the unit, said, "We're behind the plow and in the army now!" He believed, as understood by the reporter interviewing him, that the state militia, whose training he praised, had transformed into "the finest civilian army," with the responsibility of assisting the regular army in every way possible. Meeting twice a week in Memorial Hall in Gridley, the unit received lectures on tactics, chemical warfare and military communication. Regularly, the men went to the Gridley Rifle Range to improve their shooting accuracy, practiced jujitsu and participated in miniature war game scenarios. Apparently, the men enjoyed the responsibility and camaraderie, for Bassett claimed, "We may miss the old fireside and slippers once or twice a week after a hard day's work, but we would miss far more the familiar cadence [in marching], 'Hut-Two-Three-Four' every Monday and Wednesday."[32]

A vibrant Shasta County unit of the state militia also existed throughout the war. Many of its members, workers at Shasta Dam, found time on the weekends to participate in the training and sponsored activities. The *Headtower* newsletter, published regularly at the dam site, offered an incentive for signing up for the militia; it read:

> *Andy Anderson, our paint foreman, is one of the commanding officers of the Redding State Militia. According to Andy, it is an up-and-coming organization. Uniforms, equipment, etc. are furnished. Every able-bodied man between 18 and 60 is eligible and although the benefits are too numerous to describe here, Andy will gladly give all the details to anyone that is interested.*[33]

Chapter 4

WAR BONDS AND FOOD

WAR BONDS

Beginning in 1942, it was expected that the American public would support the war effort by purchasing war bonds sanctioned by the Department of the Treasury. A series of war bond (loan) drives, eight in all, raised billions of dollars, with local "war loans auctions" sponsored enthusiastically throughout the North State. The fifth war loan drive occurred between June 12 and July 8, 1944, just one week after the D-Day landing at Normandy. A special national radio presentation helped launched the drive, with President Franklin Roosevelt speaking and actor Orson Welles emceeing the event listened to by millions of Americans. In the North State, Shasta County sponsored its war loan auction in July, making it a family event, hosting a July 8 gathering and a seven o'clock affair of fun and games, including a "sensational kiddie pet parade." The outside affair, between Market and California Streets in Redding, brought in enough money to meet expectations. Participation proved successful when event officials offered free ice cream to any adult and child willing to bring their pet, courtesy of McColl's Ice Cream Company. A street dance followed the parade with music by Johnny Clark and his orchestra. For further inducement, citizens learned that special food items such as hams, potatoes and canned fruit would be sold at low prices, no ration stamps required. Nationwide, the U.S. Treasury's goal for this war bond event of raising $16 billion was met and exceeded.[34]

Captioned "He Gives 100%, You Can Lend 10%," this war bond advertisement appeared in 1943. North State citizens did their best to invest in war bonds on a regular basis, helping the region reach most of its war bond goals. *Library of Congress.*

Special war bond events surfaced now and then throughout the North State, usually as part of state and national efforts to support the announced monetary goals. In Marysville, in early June 1942, Tarzan Jr.—Johnny Sheffield, of movie fame—rode into town sitting on an army tank that was carried by a heavy-duty truck. The American Legion organization sponsored the event, having the Chinese Drum and Bugle Corps lead a short parade to the community's State Theater. Sheffield, eleven years old, spoke to a gathered crowd, including many young persons, shouting, "Keep buying, and keep 'em flying." He explained that he started in the movies at age seven and thoroughly enjoyed his new role as Tarzan Jr., losing his fear of exotic animals and learning how to swing through trees from his movie father, Johnny Weissmuller.[35]

VICTORY GARDENS

By the middle of 1942, it was clear that American farms could not keep up with the military and civilian demands for food, especially fruits and vegetables. In addition, our allies, especially Great Britain, counted on continued American food products to feed their people. On March 1, 1943, the government rationed canned fruits and vegetables, forcing hungry families to limit their consumption; at the same time, residents were asked by local officials to produce small, personal vegetable plots and to plant fruit trees in their backyards. In this way, more commercially grown food would go to the war effort and more tins could go to war use, with the added incentive of eating freshly grown food products.

To support this effort, local North State counties asked farm advisors to devise plans for helping implement a new program of "victory gardens" that would supplement the use of rationing stamps. Soon, local newspapers were running columns devoted to tips and instructional diagrams, visibly highlighting some aspects of growing crops and trees: watering, pruning, fertilizing and pest control. One such column appeared in the *Oroville Mercury-Register* in July 1943, when advertisement support for planting victory gardens gained recognition nationwide. The column, Today's Victory Garden, began with a detailed graph showing the results from properly planted parsnips, alongside a parsnip planted in poorly prepared soil. The column writer, Dean Halliday, warned readers that parsnips have a long growing season and sometimes growers become impatient; they should leave the healthy plant in the ground until winter, he said, noting that summer watering is a key to success, along with deeply prepared soil. Details such as suggesting a covering of straw to reduce the stress of possible winter freezing added to the helpful tips afforded new victory garden farmers.

At the end of the war in Europe, in 1945, large newspaper ads encouraged North State families to continue tending to their backyard gardens. In May that year, as the world learned that Germany had surrendered, one advertisement read,

> *It's easy to think of your Victory Garden as just a little plot, not amounting to much in food production. But—do you know that last year America's little Victory Gardens, like yours, produced more than eight million tons of food? That was a big help in relieving the overworked farmer and the food-packing plants. Let's do it again this year.*[36]

With the hopeful possibility that a Japanese surrender loomed imminently in August 1945, local newspapers loudly published the good news "Gas, Some Food off Ration," with details to follow as soon as possible. This announcement came as great news to war-weary North State residents eager to leave behind the deprivations of the Great Depression and World War II. In fact, the news proved intoxicating, literally, as residents finally felt that the official end of the global war had come. In Oroville, expectations from local residents reading recent updates from the OPA were that "gas, tires, shoes, fuel oil, automobiles, and a few other items" would soon be available without rationing.[37] However, government sources warned local citizens not to expect immediate relief and that "meats, sugar, and fats" would remain rationed for the time being.

Food preservation became a hot topic, and federal, state and local programs flourished throughout the war, often encouraging peoples' efforts through full-length newspaper articles or local demonstrations on effective methods of canning, dehydration and freezing. One of the most popular and successful approaches to saving food resources involved inviting state or regional "food preservation experts," often women, to present a talk or actual canning demonstration of specific foods. In this endeavor, Shasta and Tehama Counties pooled their resources, inviting Beth Campbell to come and stay for an extended time. Campbell, assigned to the North State by the University of California Agriculture Extension Service, planned to offer regular food preservation sessions, as either group presentations or private tutelage. Based at Shasta County's Farm Advisor Office on Placer Street, Campbell announced her willingness to participate in whatever venues local residents felt most comfortable with and that her services were free of product fees or other charges.

As the war progressed, pressure mounted for ever-increasing quotas of food to be produced and preserved. James Lewis, a member of the Improvement Club of Shasta County, noted, "This year [1944], more than ever before, the need for preserving food at home is urgent." He went on to claim that canned fruit and vegetables "must be set aside for our armed forces, lend-lease, and the liberated countries." "Lend-lease" refers to America's commitment to lend or lease war materials and food to countries fighting the Axis powers; early on in the war, England, fighting alone against Hitler, needed huge amounts of food and war materials. Toward the end of the war, this policy of lend or lease extended to Italy, Belgium and France.

Major concerns arose about the number of food preservation attempts that ended with failure due to improper preserving techniques, resulting in spoilage or, in some cases, poisoning. Growers and distributors in the Red Bluff area advertised the outstanding qualities of Golden Jubilee peaches as excellent for canning preservation; the Grant Merrill Orchards in Red Bluff perfected the growing and timing of the freestone variety of peaches, ensuring sweet, full-bodied development at the time of canning. Plums and apricots also remained high on the list of fruits canned throughout the North State.

During the war, Shasta Union High School, in Redding, offered rooms for developing a community-canning center. The center remained open to residents throughout the North State; all persons were welcomed to use the "facilities and instruction." Formal classes usually began in the morning, at eight thirty, demonstrating a variety of techniques for canning meats and vegetables, including chicken and string beans.

One interesting aspect of food saving involved the government's attempt to round up used vegetable oils, kitchen fats and animal fat. In the middle of the war, one ad explained, "We need all the FATS and OILS our farms and ranches can supply and all that we can salvage in American households to make more than half a million items of war equipment." Without specifically naming what war materials were made with fats, the ad did admit that the fats and oils were "vital ingredients" and that local government programs promised cash and point payments for anyone turning in fats and oils. A key ingredient of fats is glycerin, which, at the time, was used in the production of explosive devices; amazingly, it was estimated that a single pound of fat could result in the

These Red Cross volunteers canning peaches during World War II typify scenes played out in many North State kitchens throughout the conflict. Home canning reached a peak during the turning point of 1943, when an estimated 4.1 billion jars were canned. *Library of Congress.*

chemical construction of one pound of explosive material. Local North State housewives were asked to bring their fats and oils to nearby butcher shops or food plants, where government officials then collected the material and sent it to army collection centers and, finally, on to processing plants;

reworked into useful chemical forms, the fat derivatives eventually ended up in war ammunition factories. The going price for fat remained at four cents per pound for much of the war years.

Later, at the end of 1943, the federal government added an incentive, supplying two ration point credits for each pound of fat delivered.[38] Also, that same year, Judge Elmer Robinson, chairperson for the fats and grease state committee, toured the North State, visiting Oroville in the summer. In meetings with city officials and citizens, he encouraged families to pay particular attention to meat fat, suggesting many ways "waste fat" could be used at home—and then, only then, should the waste fat be brought to a local grocery store or recognized collection center. He went on, "We are not asking people to give anything they can use…but only for what would otherwise be waste." In a reminder of the important role fats and grease played in ammunition production, Robinson stated that one tablespoon of grease was enough to help make five bullets. As if to emphasize the point, he claimed that fat recycling, at this period in the war, now resided as a top priority. Focusing on "housewives," he concluded, "If every housewife does her part, there is no question that our boys on various fronts will be able to do theirs."[39]

Hoarding

From the beginning, a plethora of local, state and federal government media communications warned North State families not to hoard food items deemed necessary for the war effort. Overall, indications point to the fact that the North State followed the patriotic route and followed the guidelines on rationing and hoarding. However, as one author noted, "Some people's anxiety over food shortages and inadequate nutrition led to hoarding; especially of coffee, sugar, and red meat, which further contribute to shortages."[40] Hoarding became taboo and subject to community ridicule. Take, for example, the case of a North State woman who walked into her local store and asked to buy "two cases of canned milk." The curious clerk raised an eyebrow, suspicious of such a large order, and asked the patron why she needed that unusual amount of milk. She replied, "I want it for my dog." The grocery clerk immediately refused to proceed. The story made it into the local newspaper, with the editor furious over the incident, writing, "Isn't it high time to make people like this realize…that we are at war…that babies and growing children need the milk?"

Prices stabilized during the war as government intervention and Office of Price Administration (OPA) efforts proved effective. By 1943, local newspapers were advertising "ceiling prices" for specific food items, guaranteeing effective dates of enforcement. Grocery store owners could be prosecuted for violating the price limits and for not advertising in their ads which food items were affected. Sometimes, local North State grocery stores focused their specials on specific food groups, such as the Purity Store in Oroville when it advertised, "Salad Days Are Victory Days," offering low-price deals: one bunch of carrots for seven cents, two pounds of tomatoes for twenty-three cents, ten pounds of potatoes for thirty-nine cents and three pounds of lemons for fifty-four cents. By the middle of the war, coffee became widely available again, selling for as low as eighteen cents per pound.

FARMING

The federal government looked to North State farmers to increase their production of key agricultural goods. This process started during the middle to late years of the Great Depression, helping to supply both civilian and military needs. One big push included expanding and promoting Future Farmers of America (FFA). High schools played a prominent role in encouraging teens to get involved in local chapters of the organization. In 1944, Floyd Bidwell and Morris Doy, from the mountain community of Hat Creek, received national recognition for their efforts in the FFA (McArthur chapter). Fall River Joint Union High School district superintendent George Roehr noted, "We are proud but not surprised that Bidwell and Doty were recommended. It is just further evidence of the quality of work accomplished by the boys under the advisership of J.W. Bequette, director of vocational agriculture."

All North State farmers received notice to fill out Food-for-Freedom farm registration forms. Information acquired from these forms helped regional and federal U.S. Department of Agriculture (USDA) officials plan a "blueprint" for projecting crop production and rationing. Farmers outlined their needs for labor and necessary supplies, machinery and buildings. Harry Paxton served as chair of the Shasta County USDA.

Acquiring new farm machinery proved difficult, as one 1943 article made clear.

How very scarce new farm machinery will be in 1943 is indicated by the California quotas released from Washington last week. To be rationed by the local farm machinery rationing boards in the 57 agricultural counties of the state are 76-grain drills, 48 manure spreaders, 916 wheel-type tractors, 82 cream separators, 7-grain binders, and 34 ensilage cutters…. Of some type of machinery, such as stationary grain threshers, there will be none whatever.[41]

From Butte County, the report broke down the specific machines, which included only one spreader, thirteen wheel-type tractors, twelve milking machines, two separators, four tractor mowers and two delivery rakes. From this allotment, the local Butte County farm machinery rationing committee would determine priority in the distribution process. Despite the difficult situation of early 1943, the article noted that the federal government was moving to give farm machinery production an AA-1 preference rating, making it more likely that quotas would improve over time. To encourage increased meat production, the government in January 1943 raised the ceiling price for the sale of domestic fowl, increasing income for farmers by 20 percent. At the same time, the OPA limited the slaughtering of beef and pork during the first three months of the year to 70 percent of the previous year, making it more difficult for families to purchase meat products regularly, depending on one's county location.

The 1942 crop report, coming out in 1943, noted, for Butte County, a gross income of over $22 million, $9 million more than in 1941. However, the report cautioned that these figures represented gross receipts and that net results appeared, unofficially, less than in the previous year, due to "increased production costs." Breaking down the report, Oroville's orange and olive crop alone brought in $2 million, with olive production jumping five times higher despite the crop selling for less per ton. Poultry almost doubled as the demand for chicken products skyrocketed, while rice exploded to become Butte County's most valuable crop, earning over $3 million, a rise in value of over $1.5 million as planted acreage almost doubled.

With food demand rising as the war expanded overseas, pressure built up between the government price setting and deduction orders. Bean growers throughout the North State protested, in April 1944, crop yield prices and deductions set by the Food Distribution Administration. At a tense meeting of the growers, S. Atwood McKeehan called for direct interaction between local and regional government representatives regarding communication and discussion of prices. The key issue here centered on stabilizing demand and prices. Back in Chicago at this time, the American Farm Bureau Federation recommended a conference to help set up viewpoints from all interested parties "so that prices of such commodities may be stabilized" and to have "an effective system of price supports, including mandatory [government] commodity loans."[42]

Meanwhile, during the same month, April, peach growers, meeting in Marysville, worried over "grave problems" concerning delays in acquiring sufficient numbers of trucks (due to lack of tires) and drivers. One representative suggested looking more closely at using nearby train facilities to ship the peaches to Stockton or San Jose, where refrigeration plants might hold the crops longer as more trucks became available in those areas. Representatives from the railroad agreed to work on accomplishing the common goal of getting the fruit delivered to appropriate destinations. Of course, this in itself was a concern, as all items shipped by railroad resided under a given priority government status. Other orchard owners noted the need for hemp rope for "handling of the peach crop."

LOCAL EMPLOYMENT

Job openings, so difficult to find during the Great Depression, now became difficult to fill. Montgomery Wards learned early on that they needed to advertise far and wide around the North State to fill even the most basic job categories, such as sales of retail merchandising. One ad read, "Opportunity of rapid advancement. High school graduate preferred. If you are now employed in an essential industry or anticipate being drafted in the near future, please do not apply."

WOMEN IN THE LOCAL WORKFORCE

As the war entered the mid-1942 months, demands for more workers multiplied as California's Bay Area erupted into a massive war production center. The lure of good-paying jobs convinced many North State women to respond, moving the short distance to the East Bay, San Jose or San Francisco. With the Kaiser Shipyards gearing up to assemble a Pacific fleet of merchant vessels and warships, job openings appeared constantly in local newspapers.

Young North State men and women moved out of the area to work in Southern California for large aircraft plants, such as Lockheed in Burbank and Convair in San Diego. The Burbank plant sprawled out over a large

"I've found the job where I fit best!"

FIND YOUR WAR JOB
In Industry – Agriculture – Business

North State newspapers and national magazines constantly ran advertisements from the Bay Area for industrial job openings. Local agricultural jobs also remained plentiful, particularly in food processing plants. *Library of Congress.*

area, highlighting and perfecting a fully mechanized assembly line by June 1943.[43] Two locals, Lorena and Bill Hamilton, brother and sister, worked for Lockheed after attending Shasta Union High School, coming home to the North State when possible to visit their parents and friends.

Women also took over many of the prewar jobs in local towns of the North State counties. Ideal Laundry, in Redding, constantly advertised for women workers, explaining that no experience was necessary and the "union conditions" ensured good pay and a decent working environment.

Volunteer work for women became almost a required occupation during the war. With North State advertisements blaring the slogan "You're a Citizen Soldier: When You Do the Red Cross Work," women learned the many vital roles they could play in wartime medicine. An ad presented by the Tide Water Associated Oil Company declared that millions of surgical dressings were made for the army by American Red Cross volunteer workers in 1943, explaining that the War Department expected to raise the need for 1944. The extensive advertisement delineated the many participatory roles women could play in the Red Cross, including producing surgical dressings, serving in local canteens or hospitals, assisting

ENROLL TODAY AS A RED CROSS VOLUNTEER NURSE'S AIDE
YOUR HELP CAN SAVE MANY LIVES . . . FIND THE TIME . . . GIVE IT NOW
Call Your Red Cross Chapter or Local Civilian Defense Volunteer Office

From the beginning of the war, the Red Cross played a vital and ongoing role in the North State's support of the home front. While many young women agreed to serve in Red Cross positions outside of the North State, hundreds more consistently worked to increase awareness of programs within their local communities. *Library of Congress.*

in recreation activities for wounded soldiers or becoming a nurse's aide or home nurse trainee. It is amazing to recall that during the war, thirty-seven million women participated as Red Cross volunteers, not only serving in the capacities noted above but also raising $785 million through special local and regional fundraising efforts. On another note, a little-known fact is that a Junior Red Cross organization, which began earlier in the war, ballooned to twenty million young persons, aged twelve to seventeen. They collected and produced clothing, toys and furniture and assisted Red Cross workers when needed.[44]

In the city of Redding, the local chapter of the American Red Cross opened night classes at the local high school to train volunteer citizens, male and female, on medical treatment during emergencies. The ten two-hour class sessions included a final examination, which, if passed, was recognized with an official certificate. One Red Cross representative explained the need for this class by stating, "Facts have shown that more damage is done by untrained people handling accident cases than by the accidents themselves"[45]—a point well taken. Yuba City physician Romayne Whitney confirmed what everyone already knew: a rapid drawdown of medical personnel, doctors, nurses and medical assistants had left the North State without sufficient resources to deal with civilians. He went on to encourage "mothers and grandmothers to learn the home treatment methods of another age for application in minor cases."[46]

Small towns also participated early in the war effort to support Red Cross services. The town of Biggs, in the southern portion of Butte County, hosted a meeting in which a Red Cross representative from nearby Gridley presented suggestions from the San Francisco Red Cross office on methods for securing bandages and preparing dressings for cutting and rolling. In addition, women learned the need to make and gather bedding, especially quilts for emergency use. In the small town of Live Oak, in June 1942, members of the Grange Home Economics Club met at the home of Mrs. H.R. Turner for a potluck affair and to announce an ongoing project to make quilts for county emergency beds. The quilts made by the Biggs group, though few in number, would be added to the supplies already being prepared in Gridley and Chico, the idea being that countywide materials would become part of a comprehensive regional drive to have on hand all necessary medical supplies for use wherever they might be needed, a truly united effort.

Throughout the North State, coordinated county Red Cross defense plans surged during the rest of December 1941. Tehama County announced it had expanded its personnel and materials to meet any emergency. Designated emergency shelters, already in place from previous flooding incidents, along with food and clothing for 1,500 persons, stood ready to satisfy immediate needs. In the little town of Cottonwood, Al Green, president of the local chamber of commerce, asked all current residents in and around the town to register immediately. His committee on defense began to organize subcommittees to address any fire and nursing needs. To his grateful surprise, Green announced that fifty local men, women and high school students had signed up as plane spotters. This response proved sufficient for two women to serve during the daylight hours, while two men came on duty at night, allowing each pair of observers to limit their requirement to two nights a month. Even small towns such as Los Molinos set up their own "aircraft listening posts." In Gerber, citizens met at the local fire hall to discuss how to organize a defense committee to address emergencies, medical or otherwise. Discussions concluded that an advisory council should first be formed due "to the complexity of the activities involved." For emergency signaling, such as for blackouts, Corning decided to use a combination of ringing the fire hall bell and the "intermittent blowing of sirens," signaling all citizens to "shut off their lights"; a separate continuous blowing of the siren signaled an all-clear situation. Other volunteer roles for women opened: regular blood donor, civilian defense worker and coordinating the salvaging of metal, paper and rubber. Often, women served in more than one capacity: for example, Red Cross volunteer and airplane spotter.

As noted above, Bay Area war industries attempted to recruit women workers in the North State. The United States Employment Service, operating an office from 1407 California Street in Redding, regularly called for men and women to work in the ever-growing war industry plants in Marin County, especially Sausalito. It did not matter if the persons possessed the requisite skills to work as pipefitters, sheet metal workers, installation machinists and electricians, as the employing companies offered lucrative contracts under which new employees began by working with experienced and skilled persons—men and women. Of course, accepting one of these employment offers meant finding hard-to-obtain housing, although some companies offered free cafeteria meals, which helped. Often, women moving to the Bay Area bunked two or more to a room, saving on rent by giving up privacy.

Rationing

Residents learned early in the war that rationing would become a way of life. Adults and children over five years old, coming off years of food deprivation during the Great Depression, understood what rationing meant, but it was still difficult to understand how the system, during wartime, would work.

One of the first items rationed was automobile tires. Rubber sources in Asia now came under Japanese control, so the government asked everyone to conserve rubber. In Shasta County, the rationing board put out a notice that citizens would need to apply for special certificates to buy new tires. North State residents learned that each county received a small allotment of tires and each rationing board would control the distribution of each tire. Interested buyers needed to pay a fee for the right to purchase the tire and then pay the price of the tire. During the last weeks of 1941, only six permits received validation in Shasta County, with one permit given to William Stevenson, a contractor, who needed three truck tires. Early on in the rationing process, with tires at a premium, some theft did occur. W.H. Reading reported a wire wheel tire and tube stolen from his garage on Center Street in Redding; stealing now became a patriotic issue, and if the responsible party received punishment, it was usually harsh.

Butte County had its share of tire thefts during the first half of 1942, with one newspaper report claiming a rise in those persons stealing tires of 50 percent from the same time the previous year. Patriotic responses to curb the problem resulted in lots of suggestions, some good, some bad, always recommending strict punishment for violators. In Oroville, one newspaper editorial warned car owners "to take extra precautions to safeguard those precious possessions [tires]." The editorial recommended keeping cars out of sight when possible, suggesting a locked garage as the best alternative. Other residents wanted to fight the problem from the other end of the crime, severely punishing anyone found guilty of tire theft, hinting that the crime "becomes a compounded offense, far worse than mere theft" and firmly stating, "The rogues who steal tires during the war-born shortage deserve no leniency."[47]

Another issue that regularly appeared as a link to tire use or misuse was speeding. Jackrabbit starts, hard braking and, generally, high-speed driving reduced tire tread wear faster than normal; of course, road conditions played a huge role, as well. The idea of promoting good driving habits spread around the North State, and speeding became a central cause of disagreement, with patriotic news editorials claiming, "The fellow who is

Tire rationing significantly affected the North State economy during the entire war. Counties set up elaborate legal processes to apply for new tires; the system established priorities for agricultural requests and service-related businesses (e.g., plumbers, contractors). *Library of Congress.*

needlessly burning up the highway would be fighting mad if someone would question his patriotism." Local law enforcement urged drivers to plan their driving time to adjust to slower speeds and gentle braking—coasting to a stop with only minimal use of the brake pedal. Hurrying, except in cases of emergency, would be no excuse. On the enforcement side, one editorial suggested an appropriate punishment.

> *Besides the usual fine or jail sentence, they* [judges] *might add the condition that the speeder purchase $1 worth of defense stamps for every mile over the legal limit as a reminder that he hasn't been playing fair with his country.*[48]

In Oroville, business owners and others reported few reserves of tires in the area. Roy Gault, a new and used car dealer, reported a sales slump of 7 percent one month after Pearl Harbor. Another car dealer, Paul West, said that he could obtain tires for critical war-related deliveries but not for other civilian retail products; in frustration, he remarked, "I may have to go out and steal a horse." In the lumber business, William Brown of Sterling Lumber summed up the situation, "We just can't get tires....We'll run higher loads and avoid small deliveries of lumber." Even the division manager for PG&E in Oroville admitted, "We don't have any spare tires for our machines, because we have been buying locally and 'knew' that we didn't need to build up a reserve."[49]

Tires became such an issue by mid-July 1943 that local tire experts worked on special civilian contracts to train army personnel on proper tire use and care. John Heinrich of Oroville traveled throughout the Bay Area military bases, to Reno and also to the new Camp Beale base near Marysville, conducting daylong instructional sessions, showing participants how to properly recap a worn tire, teaching them how to distinguish different types of irregular wear and offering suggestions for repair. Working through a variety of different-sized rims and wheels, Heinrich covered lightweight jeeps and heavyweight army trucks and personnel carriers. During the rationing of tires in the early and middle years of the war, local North State drivers desiring new tires needed to include in their application request a compilation of their tire inspection records—no records, no new tires.[50]

Early in the war, car dealers, especially used car dealers, attempted to sell their remaining stock of automobiles as soon as possible. In late December 1941, C.F. Kylling Company in Marysville noted: "Every car priced to move." Used vehicles ranged from a 1931 Ford sedan priced low at $89 to a 1936 Plymouth Deluxe four-door touring sedan—sporting aluminum alloy pistons, full-length water jackets, hydraulic brakes, a safety steel body, chair-height seats and an eighty-two-horsepower motor—for $259. The highest-priced car, at $679, was a 1939 Dodge coup with a heater and radio.

By June 1942, businesses in every Northern California county were feeling the impact of the war. In Yuba City, the Kiwanis Club sponsored a regional meeting to discuss issues limiting or hurting production and sales. Orlin Harter, owner of a local canning company, divulged that the reduced allotments of tin for food containers limited canning production, noting also that the local labor supply had by then, June, dwindled to around half of what it was before the war. As far as making it to market with finished products, mostly canned fruit from local orchards, the government "earmarked" 32 percent of production for "war uses."

Ration books, usually printed in red, blue and green, held a series of approved stamps for a designated consumer product, including food items. Printers placed images of ships, airplanes, tanks, guns and horns of

With the coming of February 1942, major automakers discontinued making new automobiles for domestic civilian consumption; instead they quickly retooled to produce war vehicles. Chrysler Corporation diversified its production, making aircraft engines, tanks and personnel carriers. The automobile depicted above, an Oldsmobile B-44, appearing in a North State newspaper advertisement, became one of the last prewar vehicles available to the public. *From the* Gridley Herald.

Keeping their automobile running challenged drivers as service parts became unavailable. Advertisements like the one above reminded North State drivers of the responsibility they incurred in maintaining their car, either at home, at their local service station or, in this case, at the local Chevrolet dealer. *From the* Gridley Herald.

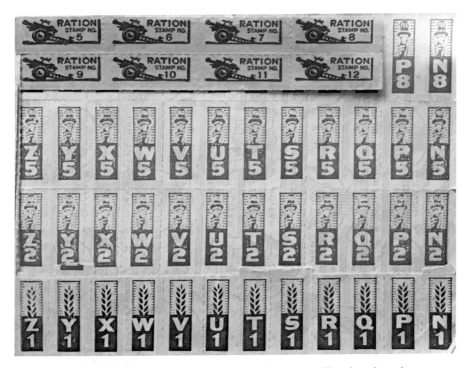

The idea behind World War II ration stamps centered on controlling the sale and distribution of food and other commodities that were in short supply due to the war. Red stamps were used when buying meat and butter, and the buyer used blue stamps for processed foods. *Author's collection.*

plenty on the stamps, which sometimes also displayed a torch of liberty. Newspapers carried notices of stamps and items still declared valid by the OPA. For example, in July 1944, one notice declared, "Meats, Fats, Etc.—Book 4 red stamps A8 through Z8 valid indefinitely." Another item, sugar, remained limited for purchase, with five pounds being the upper limit; an additional five pounds could be purchased if used for canning purposes, using "Stamp 40." A-12 coupons were, by 1944, still limiting gasoline to three gallons.

Early in the war, the government offered defense stamps as a way for low-income families to help support the war effort. For as little as twenty-five cents in change, a person could purchase a stamp, which they then pasted into a savings book. Civilian organizations often helped sponsor stamp-selling events. After accumulating seventy-five stamps, the filled stamp book was worth $25, even though your investment totaled $18.75, bonds matured years later. This proved to be a boon for the federal government, as everyone was expected to participate.[51] The Oroville School District continually sponsored "defense stamp drives," with initial efforts proving quite successful in hitting their goals. In one week of January 1942, the school district raised $89.60. An excited superintendent, Clarence Fylling, responded by commenting, "It is planned to sell the stamps each Thursday," adding, "It is anticipated that the number of persons purchasing the stamps and the amount will increase."[52]

RECYCLING DRIVES

North State families received constant reminders to save and recycle key materials—called "salvaging" during World War II—and tin became one of the first items salvaged. At the beginning of the war, confusion reigned as families tried to understand the myriad of advertisements attempting to instruct them how tin should be recycled. By mid-1942, newspaper ads were complaining that not enough tin was being collected during a specific period known as a "tin drive." One advertisement explained the proper procedure:

As early as January 10, 1942, the government asked homeowners and farmers to join in a "Salvage for Victory" campaign, listing tin and other metals as a top priority for war materials. Due to the resulting tin shortage, North State residents discovered that many formerly canned goods now came packaged in alternative materials. *Library of Congress.*

From the beginning of hostilities, the War Department let the government know that vital raw materials were needed to succeed in war production. To this end, local communities responded to salvage "drives," running ads in newspapers asking citizens to gather aluminum, silk, cooking fat, iron, steel and rubber. *National Archives.*

To prepare tin cans for salvage, the housewife should remove the label, cut out both top and bottom, wash and dry the can, and flatten it by stepping on it. The two ends may be slipped inside the flattened can....Deliver them to the retail food stores.[53]

Other items requested for recycling included iron, rubber and metals of all types. Volunteers stationed at various collection points in towns separated and weighed items; one major collection location existed "opposite the Redding Theatre."

PRICES

Christmas 1941 (right after the Pearl Harbor attack) revealed prices as usual, as it was too late to change rates for items shipped and awaiting purchase in stores. Many of these holiday-type products became scarce and more expensive as the war years moved along. However, in 1941, in Red Bluff, one store offered Christmas tree lights in strings of fifteen bulbs—each "light burns individually"—for $2; that was an expensive item for the average family. Photo albums, designed as presents, went for $1.25, while leather wallets averaged just over $1.

The consumer, interestingly enough, saw rationing on certain items yet discovered excellent non-ration products on sale all through the war. JCPenney advertised specials constantly, particularly in the area of women's

BULK FOOD VALUES

You save money when you buy good foods in bulk—the cost of an expensive can or package. Top quality beans, rice, lentils, etc., scientifically packed under the most rigid sanitary conditions are the kind you get at Safeway.

RICE	Blue Rose Long Grain	1 lb. cello	12c	3-lb. cello	35c
RICE	M. L. B.	1 lb. pkg.	13c	2-lb. pkg.	24c

Vermicelli	Colloseum Semo 16 oz. cello pkg.	13c	Split Peas	Green and yellow 1 lb. pkg.	12c
Macaroni	& Spaghetti, Collo- seum, 2 lb. pkg.	23c	Soup Mix	Minute Man Assorted, 2½ oz. pkg.	3-25c
Noodles	Colosseum, Fine Wide, 12 oz. pkg.	14c	Soup Mix	Rancho Noodle 2½ oz. pkg.	3-25c
Walnuts	Diamond Large 1 lb. cello bag	32c	Henderoni	Van Camp's 6 oz. pkg.	3-27c

The Safeway store in Gridley offered the prices shown above in a 1943 newspaper advertisement. Price continuity remained stable between most stores in the North State, with limits placed on prices by the Office of Price Administration. *From the* Gridley Herald.

clothing. For example, one ad in 1944 offered "cool, washable, Brentwood cotton dresses" for as little as $1.98, in a variety of sizes; the dress featured "stitched pockets" and "kick pleats." This was the lead sale item, whereas the store's regular-priced items included wool slacks for $3, skirts for $2 and girls' striped sweaters for $0.75.

President Roosevelt issued Executive Order 8875 authorizing the creation of a huge government organization, the Office of Price Administration (OPA), to control the price range of food and other items, prevent inflation and organize a rationing system of food and needed war materials. The OPA regularly sent out nationwide notices of "ceiling prices" for food items, expecting that local food outlets would follow. The goal was to achieve nationwide stabilization of consumer prices, allowing all sections of the country to benefit. In the North State, toilet paper typically sold for seventeen cents for three large rolls; the same price applied to waxed paper (used to wrap sandwiches and other food items), but it came in a single 125-foot roll. Canned fruits and vegetables ranged in price, with fruit cocktails low at fourteen cents, corn at seventeen cents, string beans at nineteen cents and peas at twenty cents.

Interestingly, early in the war, North State shoppers continued to have access to oysters, shredded coconut, tuna, sliced pineapple, and canned ravioli, the latter selling for twenty-two cents for a sixteen-ounce jar. Coffee did arrive in sufficient quantities in North State stores, which sold one-pound packages of whole beans for a low price of twenty cents and a high of thirty-two cents for MJB-brand coffee sold in a glass jar—all coffee sales required ration stamps in addition to the money.

Chapter 5

ENTERTAINMENT, HOUSING
AND EDUCATION

Have intended to write you for quite some time
as I have missed the hometown news.
—*Seabee officer Frank Lord of Redding*

LEISURE TIME AND HOLIDAYS

During the war, North State residents did their best to deal with the hot summers. Air-conditioning, rare in most buildings, proved expensive to run and prone to breakdowns. Residents living near the Sacramento River enjoyed picnicking and swimming in the many riverfront parks, sitting happily under the thick branches of abundant oak or cottonwood trees. During the war years, Redding planned to construct and maintain a postwar municipal plunge for Caldwell River Park, using the cool Sacramento River waters and developing picnic and entertainment areas.

From the earliest months of 1942, each county in the North State devoted personnel and resources toward building civic pride and a sense of common commitment. Enacted differently at times, one type of event appeared in all counties: community picnic celebrations. Usually, town planners, men and women, prepared activities for the entire family, especially focusing on fun games for children as a means to distract from their continual confrontation and the ongoing stress of dealing with war news. Hoop-ringing games rated high as joint parent and child competitions. Often, a small charge to participate helped pay for the food offerings or went into a community fund for the next war bond drive. Hot dogs, ice cream and sodas, always a favorite, brought in additional money. Richard Mallery, the serving chairperson for the 1944 celebration in Shasta County, received permission to offer defense stamps for the winners of the various games and competitions. Community picnics became so successful that they earned a reputation as monthly extensions of the traditional Fourth of July picnics.

Fourth of July celebrations took on special meaning during the war years as patriotic demonstrations, with community officials strongly suggesting that all citizens attend. And so it was, on July 4, 1944, in Lake Redding Park, when over five thousand persons arrived to celebrate and participate. At that time, Redding mayor Ivan Dunlap dedicated the new city pavilion, located at the park; over eight hundred people danced the night away on the newly laid floor.

Movie Theaters

Older adults and young people ran off to the movies, possibly because they wanted to escape the work and stress that dominated their everyday lives, possibly because one of their favorite Hollywood stars appeared in the newspaper advertisement and perhaps even because it was simply something different to do. Escaping the day-to-day stress of a new wartime environment did prove a major impetus for moviegoing, and Shasta County families flocked to the movies regularly. The Cascade Theatre offered a variety of movies, opening at times for matinees and evening showings. After the war began, movies such as *Flying Cadets* interested viewers as they showcased young men learning how to fly and prepare for combat engagements in aerial dogfights. Along the lines of this script, the State Theatre in Red Bluff screened the latest Warner Brothers war film, *International Squadron*, starring Ronald Reagan, future California governor and president of the United States. Reagan played an American stunt pilot looking for adventure in the Britain's Royal Air Force. These early movies predicted more American involvement in the war effort against the Axis powers.

In 1943, at the State Theatre in Oroville, large crowds watched Noël Coward's *In Which We Serve*, encouraged by the excellent reviews from major city newspapers; one newspaper advertisement teased, "It Can't Be Told! It Must Be Seen." Coward played the leading role, Captain "D" of HMS *Torrin*, a British destroyer. Coward and some of his men make it

The Cascade Theater in Redding opened in August 1935 and soon became a prime entertainment destination for the entire family. With seating of over 1,300, it proudly offered air-conditioning—the first public building in Redding to do so—along with a wide variety of movie genres. During the war years, student admission remained twenty-five cents, with an added fee of four cents for a "Defense Tax"; general admission tickets cost forty cents plus the defense tax. *Library of Congress.*

to a life raft after their ship receives a torpedo hit. Crew members, with time on their hands, recall their previous experiences with family and war events, such as the Dunkirk rescue and the Battle for Crete. Coward eloquently mixed documentary film clips with scenes from recorded movie stage filming; the result was impressive, and this film was well attended by local audiences. Once again, American moviegoers enthusiastically responded with respect for the British effort to fight against Germany and Italy alone, prior to Pearl Harbor. Oroville residents reacted so well to the movie that the State Theatre owner decided to run the film continuously from two o'clock in the afternoon onward on Fridays and Saturdays. The movie would have won the Best Picture award had it not been for another film classic, *Casablanca*, included in the competition—another movie with a war-related theme.

As the years pressed on, Hollywood continued to produce war-related movies, often comedies and usually dealing with interesting real-world home front situations. This was the case with the 1944 release of *The Miracle of Morgan's Creek*, starring Eddie Bracken and the popular Betty Hutton. In the film, Hutton, after participating in a patriotic "send-off" party, discovers she is married, but she cannot remember to which recruit. A series of funny misunderstandings follow, treating the viewer to what film critic Bosley Crowther called "a more audacious picture—a more delightfully irreverent one." The Cascade Theater in Redding ran the movie, advertising it with the catchphrase, "It's a Miracle of Entertainment." Meanwhile, the other theater in Redding, the Redding Theatre, showed an older film, *Dr. Gillespie's Criminal Case*, from 1943, with Lionel Barrymore, popular leading man Van Johnson and a young Donna Reed.

Escapism at the movies became a cherished pastime during the war. Residents, young and old, claimed their favorite male and female actors, waiting patiently for newspaper, magazine and radio announcements describing the latest Hollywood movies. Throughout the war, certain personalities guaranteed profitable attendance at theaters in Marysville, Chico, Anderson and Redding. Filmed in 1941 before Pearl Harbor, *A Yank in the RAF* (Royal Air Force) rallied American support for Britain's lone fight against Germany, as had the movie *Flying Cadets*, noted earlier. Starring Tyrone Power and Clark Cable, *A Yank in the RAF* reveals how American pilots volunteered to help in the fight.

Two hugely popular movies came out the next year as America became deeply involved in the fighting: *Casablanca* and *Mrs. Miniver*. *Casablanca*, with wonderful performances by veteran actor Humphrey Bogart and Ingrid

Mrs. Miniver, starring Greer Garson and Walter Pidgeon, filmed in 1942, came to North State audiences in 1943, showing at the Butte Theatre in Gridley, among others in the region. The film became so popular that continuous showings occurred on Sundays. *Wikipedia (public domain).*

In early 1945, the Senator Theatre in Chico sponsored a war bond drive, which, as can be seen above, was well attended. The theater opened in 1928 with silent short films and some vaudeville performances. The lobby has remained close to its original form, including period murals. *Merriam Library Digital Collections.*

Bergman, drew moviegoers into Humphrey's desperate inner struggle to become involved in helping his former lover and her fugitive husband, all while trying to placate local Vichy French authorities in Morocco, Africa, and avoid the watchful and suspicious eyes of newly arrived Nazis officers. Bogart, for his performance, won Best Actor at the 1944 Academy Awards. By the time *Casablanca* appeared in North State theaters, most Americans already fully supported the war effort, but the reminder drove home the idea that a commitment must be enduring. The same message came through loud and clear in Greer Garson and Walter Pidgeon's well-received dramatic portrayal of a wartime British family struggling to adapt to constant personal and war challenges. *Mrs. Miniver*, acclaimed for its deep commitment to showing realistically how war influenced families, allowed Garson to reveal a range of emotions while remaining steady and supportive, winning her the highly competitive Best Actress award. Pidgeon also was recognized and nominated for Best Actor, while *Mrs. Miniver*'s other awards included Best Picture, Director, Screenplay, Special Effects and Cinematography. In addition to these wins, the movie received seven nominations for other categories.

Audiences also craved movies with adventure, music and comedy. Music and comedy combined when longtime favorites Mickey Rooney and Judy Garland teamed up in 1944 to film *Girl Crazy*, which played to audiences at the Shasta Theatre and elsewhere in the North State. One of the dramatic movies for the North State and America came as the war ended. Samuel Goldwyn's classic *Best Years of Our Lives* revealed a new kind of desperate struggle, the challenge of reengaging in civilian life in America. The lives of three returning veterans highlight the difficulties of families adjusting to their fathers, brothers and friends being home again. An outstanding cast assured a strong showing, and the Academy recognized the achievement by naming it Best Movie, also awarding the film Best Director (William Wyler), Best Actor (Fredric March) and Best Supporting Actor (Harold Russell). In the film, Russell, a decorated veteran who lost the use of both hands, is given two hooks to serve as hands. The movie became a must-see experience for American families, eventually earning more money than any movie since *Gone with the Wind* in 1939.

RADIO PROGRAMS

Television did not exist during World War II. Most North State families, in search of news and entertainment, looked to the radio and newspapers. Complete radio programming for the evening hours appeared regularly in newspapers, laying out the offerings from the main radio stations, KPO, KGO, KQW and KVCV, operating at their respective assigned frequencies: 680, 810, 40 and 1230 kilocycles on the radio dial. Beginning at six o'clock in the evening and lasting until eight o'clock, broadcasts summarized the day's war news and economic and political events. *Report to the Nation* remained a popular time slot, at seven thirty; announcers reviewed the day's events and interviewed guests. At the end of the war, this program would carry President Truman's announcement of the dropping of the atomic bomb.

Entertainment radio programs varied from night to night, with personalities like Bing Crosby dominating Thursday evening at the six o'clock hour on KPO; KQW responded by airing the Dinah Shore show a half-hour later and received a high percentage of listeners. Interestingly, KGO presented *Saludos Amigos* (Greetings Friends) to Spanish-speaking audiences at nine-thirty on Thursday evenings.

KPO and KGO also carried special political events, such as the 1944 republican convention in Chicago, allowing North State residents to hear gavel-to-gavel action as the members moved to nominate Thomas Dewey of

By the start of World War II, most families listened regularly to the family radio. In this photo taken in April 1941, a family from Georgia gathers around the radio, shown on the counter by the girl standing. A wide variety of programs sequenced during any typical day, appealing to all age groups. *Library of Congress.*

New York for president; Dewey would go on to lose to Franklin D. Roosevelt, as the latter won his fourth term as president. Sunday programming on the radio began with religious services, such as *Bible School, Israel, Radio Pulpit, Tabernacle Choir* and *Catholic Hour,* but quickly changed to national and international news at eleven-thirty in the morning. *News Parade and World Today* briefed North State listeners on top stories, from war news and politics to special notices concerning changes in war rationing and draft and enlistment regulations. *War Journal, Army Hour, Fighting Front* and *America in the Air* provided news about the general movements of major armies, training updates and quick interviews with military leaders.

Besides the news, two of the most listened-to radio programs were band music and comedies. North State residents, no different from the rest of the country, wanted an entertainment venue to pull them away from the day-to-day stress of work and war news. Popular bands, such as Guy Lombardo's, played regularly on Saturday night starting at six o'clock. Programs including *Bandstand* highlighted newly discovered talent as well as veteran performers. It was common for married and courting North State couples to turn up the volume, move the sofa and chairs back against the wall and dance for an hour when *Spotlight Bands* came on **KGO** at six-thirty every Saturday night. The sheer variety of musical styles proved staggering on specifically focused radio programs, from classical orchestra concertos to foot-stomping barn dance numbers.

DANCES AND ENTERTAINMENT CENTERS

Butte County went all out to help provide servicemen and women opportunities for entertainment. In 1943, Oroville opened its municipal auditorium as a recreation center for service members stationed anywhere in the area. During the opening festivities in July, young women from Oroville and Chico volunteered for a welcoming dance; music was furnished by a local band. The auditorium, now remodeled for recreation, offered a lounge area with books, magazines and newspapers; a large open area for table

Dances gave servicemen and women an opportunity to come into Chico or Oroville to socialize and relax from the ongoing stress and challenges of training. Chico's Veteran's Memorial Hall on the Esplanade is the site of the 1944 dance shown above. Dedicated to commemorating veterans of the First World War, the site today is the Museum of Northern California Art. *Nopel Collection.*

games; and an extensive dance floor space. A coffee and donut canteen also offered cigarettes and soft drinks, sold at cost, to active service guests; open six days a week, the recreation center became a popular destination for military and civilians alike, throughout the weekends.

NEWSPAPERS

Daily or twice weekly, local newspapers informed citizens of the ongoing war in Europe and the Pacific. Believing their family members serving in the military or working in defense plants around the state and country might like to hear about local news, North State parents sent, now and then, all or portions of newspapers. One young man, Frank Lord of Redding, a Seabee officer originally stationed on one of the Aleutian Islands, received copies of the *Record-Searchlight* while in Hawaii. He wrote to the newspaper office, "Have intended to write you for quite some time as I have missed the hometown news. I received your paper when I was out before and then passed it along to some of the others from Shasta County that I met now and then. We all enjoyed it very much."

Typical city newspapers during World War II structured their printed pages in much the same format as shown opposite. The *Appeal-Democrat*, for example, on July 14, 1942, placed important international war news on the front page, leading with a headline that read "Red Capital [Moscow] Under Double Threat," splitting the other major story, "Axis Repulsed in Lunge on Egypt Corridor: RAF Defies Desert Storms," into side-by-side columns. A surprising amount of military detail is given in these Associated Press (AP) news releases, including specific geographic locations, numbers of troops involved and the names of leading military personnel, especially generals. Also on the front page, critical federal government decisions appeared, such as on this day, where one article headlined "Board Directed to Call Single Men Register First" explained that local draft boards were now directed to "call up married men last, taking single war workers before husbands and fathers." In fact, a progressive priority list was published that named the following categories in order of call-up.

Single men with no dependents;
Single men who do not contribute to the war effort but who have dependents;
Single men with dependents and who contribute to the war effort;
Married men without children who are not engaged in the war effort;

On Monday, December 8, 1941, Marysville and Yuba City residents learned more detail about the Pearl Harbor attack from their *Appeal-Democrat* newspaper. Notice the mix of international, national and local news on the front page. *From the* Appeal-Democrat.

Married men with children who are engaged in the war effort;

Married men living with wife and children or children only and who are not engaged in the war effort;

Married men living with wife and children or children only who are engaged in the war effort.

One caveat relating to the list above stated, "To be classed as a married man a registrant must have been married before December 8, 1941 and must be living with his wife or children."

The front page usually contained local stories of significance, especially if they were related to the war effort at home. On July 14, 1942, the paper ran a headline article titled "Sutter [County] Selectees Leave Wednesday," referencing thirty young men who had recently passed their final physical examinations in Sacramento and were now granted fourteen-day furloughs to "return home and conclude business affairs." Saying their final goodbyes to family and friends, these new inductees would be reporting to various training bases, some in California. On this day, it was announced that small going-away gift boxes were to be distributed containing cigarettes and candles, items usually in demand by men. The article included specific dates and times for the new soldiers to report to the bus station in Yuba City, where relatives and friends "may gather" to say goodbye.

Page 2 sported a huge JCPenney advertisement for bath towels, thirty-five cents apiece; a calendar showing local events, such as the Gridley swim party; a Marysville Christian Missionary meeting; and a Rebekah Lodge meeting. Playing card games remained popular in World War II, and a special section of this page announced open-invitation card parties and other special parties, such as the annual summer party of Sacred Heart Catholic Church in Gridley. State and more local news spread across page 3, with a special section highlighting "Twin Cities Today" (Marysville and Yuba City), which usually described the comings and goings of local citizens—most travel trips remained limited to area towns. One interesting state story covered the first known federal court case challenging President Roosevelt's executive order to intern persons of Japanese descent. Miss Mituye Endo, with her attorney, appeared in San Francisco's federal court pleading to "secure her release from the Tule Lake reception center at Newell, Calif." The article noted that Endo's brother Kunio now served in the army "and this would exempt her from detention if she was of Italian or German descent, instead of Japanese." Also on this page, the local theaters—Tower and State in Marysville and Smith in (Yuba City)—ran their advertisements; all three boasted that they were "cooled by refrigerated air" as a July inducement.

Page 4 allowed for incoming stories from neighboring small towns, such as Gridley, Biggs and Live Oak. Biggs announced that its patriotic state militia now stood at 120 men, more than any other town in Butte County. Gridley reported a hit-and-run accident on Highway 99E; the culprit clipped two boys riding their bicycles. At the hospital, doctors found no major injuries concerning the boys' physical condition, and the hospital subsequently released the boys in short order. The boys described the runaway vehicle to California Highway Patrol officers as a "dark pickup." Officials from the little town of Live Oak announced a special Live Oak

All major North State newspapers regularly printed detailed news from smaller outlying towns. This was the case with the *Appeal-Democrat*, as is shown in this reprint of page 4 of the July 14, 1942 edition. Special attention was paid by this newspaper to stories coming from Gridley, Biggs and Live Oak. Other towns covered included Wheatland, Grimes and Camptonville. *From the* Appeal-Democrat.

Junk Rally day, where local citizens could bring in their scrap "iron, steel, [and] scrap rubber" as a patriotic gesture. In addition, on this page, anyone might offer notice of specific family trips and visits, revealing the extent to which a newspaper reader might discover who was visiting whom and for what reason. It is quite amazing to think of this page as a sort of 1940s social media outlet, albeit in print form: birthday parties, broken legs and returning home from a trip are among the events described on this day. In some cases, you learned the whereabouts and health of a friend in the military on this page, as did Mr. and Mrs. Paul Andes, who learned on July 14 that their son, Lloyd, "who is somewhere in the Pacific... had to reenter the hospital for treatment of a leg infection caused by an automobile accident."

Page 5, titled the Sport Spot, revealed the extent to which North State residents participated in and followed sports, local and professional. Associated Press coverage of major league baseball, always a favorite sport, provided detailed, almost inning-by-inning news of key players and outcomes from the day before. In this case, one major article reviewed the New York Yankees' close win over the Detroit Tigers, then spent time praising lefty Washington Senators pitcher Walter Masterson's 7–0 shutout of the Cleveland Indians. Another exciting sports focus looked at the American League baseball "batting crown" (batting average), highlighting on this day how New York Yankee second baseman Joseph Gordon recorded a "perfect day" the day before, hitting two doubles and two singles to regain the batting competition with a score of .347, followed by Boston's famous Ted Williams at .343.

On local sports, a column titled the Sport Light covered local Valley League baseball games. The Marysville Giants sat "perched at the top of the Valley League standings on July 14, 1942, with only ten games to go." The most recent game featured the Chico Colts against the Marysville team, with reporting like the following:

> *Baseball fans enjoy watching base hits soar to the outer pasture and they like to see a good job of pitching, but of late, they have been applauding repeatedly the big defensive performances turned up in almost every league game. The Sunday night show here had a full share with the busy Giant infield turning in 14 assists.*[54]

Page 6 provided a myriad of entertainment information, including a complete listing of radio programs for the next day, a difficult crossword

Double Header BaseBall
Sunday — 1:30
Bryant Field
First Game, Valley League Game
Chico vs. Marysville
Second Game
Ogden Reds vs. Marysville
- - -
Admission . . . 45cents Including Tax
Men in Uniform Free to All Games
No Broadcast of This Game

If there was one sport to select that remained popular during World War II, it would be baseball. Sacramento Valley League games continued to be played on a regular basis, albeit with many of the best players away in the military. Rivalries between towns brought large crowds to many games, such as the one noted above. *From the* Appeal-Democrat.

puzzle (and answers for the previous day), a Mind Your Manners question and answer column and numerous syndicated comic "funnies" strips. The crossword topic for the day was "Early Lawmaker" and included clues such as "He was a Chief Justice of the U.S. _____ Court," and "Symbol for Selenium." The Mind Your Manners column tested the reader's knowledge of etiquette by asking questions such as "Is it good manners for a house guest who didn't bring his sugar card with him to use several spoonfuls of sugar in every cup of coffee?" The answer, of course, is no. The questions became more difficult as the reader continued.

One of the popular comic strips that appeared regularly in the Marysville paper was *Freckles and His Friends*, of which a sample is shown on

Top: World War II newspapers ran a variety of regular columns and informational diagrams to help the public understand topics related to the war. This Curious World, by W. Ferguson, ran for a long time in local North State newspapers, offering interesting facts such as the speed of a descending bomb dropped from an aircraft. *From the* Gridley Herald.

Bottom: Merrill Blosser's comic strip, *Freckles and His Friends*, began in 1915, and it remained popular throughout the World War II years. Many North State newspapers carried the comic strip, as its setting, in a small town, recalled social episodes familiar to local residents. *From the* Gridley Herald.

the bottom of the opposite page. Other well-received and regular comic strips appearing in North State newspapers included *Alley Oop*, *Boots and Her Buddies*, *The Nebbs*, *Red Ryder* and *Out Our Way*; these "strips" appeared in a variety of formats. For example, *Out Our Way* ran as a single large scene, whereas *Alley Oop* contained three frames, while *Freckles and His Friends*, as shown, always ran as four-frame scenes. To capture and retain reading audiences, these comic strips utilized ongoing adventures with climatic or mysterious last frames, enticing the reader to come back for the next part of the story. As for content, comic strips varied from war-related topics, such as sinking Japanese submarines, to food rationing and elaborate mystery murders or robberies; imaginative and engaging, these comic strips, in their unique way, diverted the reader from the everyday world of war-related stress and challenges to a fantasy world where one might find pure entertainment.

The classified section of the *Appeal Democrat* occupied page 7 on this day, along with agriculture-related stock market prices and trends. Categories for the classified section started with lost and found requests and then moved to employment opportunities, house and room rentals, real estate sales, poultry and stock, furniture and miscellaneous. An automotive category offered an opportunity to buy or sell an automobile with one local car dealer, A.W. Holtman (Buick and GM trucks) at 430 Second Street in Marysville, stating, "We pay the highest cash price for clean cars with good tires." Tires appeared as a singular concern in these ads, with one person writing, "Wanted: A Ford Coupe in good condition—must have extra good tires." Noticeably, most ads did not offer a sales price, but everyone wanted "good tires." Under "Employment Opportunities," the largest ad that day highlighted the need for carpenters in the shipbuilding industry in the San Francisco Bay Area. Offering a starting salary of $0.95 to $1.23 per hour, depending on experience, the ad claimed the only qualifications necessary were bringing proof of citizenship and being between the ages of eighteen and sixty-four. Interested applicants learned that carpenter union representatives would hold interviews on July 17 and employ "any man that is qualified." On another note, one small ad from a Japanese American citizen declared, "Having closed my business, I will not be responsible for any debts contracted by anyone other than myself after this date."

The last page of the July 14, 1942 *Appeal Democrat* contained the local editorial and special feature columns. Titled "Refreshing Facts About Rubber," the editorial recalled how much national and local attention had been focused on the shortage of rubber and the need to salvage the used material. The latest national rubber drive, in early 1942, had failed to meet the goal set by military and political officials. However, the article claimed that according to recent news reports, despite original estimates, enough reclaimed rubber had arrived to supply factories for a full year; this was in addition to the six-month supply already on hand. Reporting that rubber factories reported an excellent ratio of turning reclaimed rubber into new rubber products, the writer noted that 1.15 tons of scrapped rubber represented 1 finished ton of a new rubber product. The article also alluded to the new synthetic-rubber manufacturing plants coming into operation, mentioning newly acquired national data on tire use. As for retreaded tires, early reports revealed that retreaded tires made from reclaimed rubber gave five to ten thousand miles of service, whereas retreads made from new rubber extended the life of the tire to fifteen to twenty thousand miles. Lastly, the editor explained how many factories continued to experiment with different mixtures of new and reclaimed rubber in a variety of war-related products.

The Circus

It is quite amazing to consider all the transforming economic and social pressures of World War II on North State California. With everything focused on the fighting overseas and the constant reminders to support the home front, the public needed diverse avenues of relaxation and relief. One interesting entertainment opportunity visited the North State a couple of times each year despite the ongoing hardships of work and war; that opportunity was the circus. The Arthur Brothers Big Show Circus highlighted a traditional three-ring activity performance area, including wild animals highly trained to delight guests from the youngest age to the oldest senior. Titania, a massive, docile elephant, showcased a parade of beasts; then separate animal acts forced viewers to scan from one ring to the next. Claiming "new acts from Europe," the Arthur Brothers circus completed a two-day run in Marysville starting on June 5, 1943, with two performances a day, transforming the corner of Tenth and K Streets into a canvas-covered arena.

HOUSING

World War II brought about a nationwide shortage of housing as all available home-building materials went to war industries. However, renting rooms remained a popular option for homeowners to bring in extra monthly funds. From the earliest days of the war, Shasta County appeared to have a ready supply of homes and rooms for rent. Much of the availability resulted from several years of gearing up for the huge numbers of Shasta Dam job seekers during the latter part of the Great Depression. Amazingly, fully furnished homes appeared in daily advertisements, some ads offering electric refrigerators and "air cooling." One interesting property owner offered a less expensive option for sleeping, stating that one could rent his "large sleeping porch."

Home or room rental prices rarely appeared in newspaper advertisements, but on certain occasions, when the homeowner wanted to attract certain renters, fees were published. In one case, a two-room, furnished upstairs living quarters, including a fully functional kitchenette with an "electric refrigerator," was listed for a monthly rental fee of $28.50. This included a private bathroom. The listing read, "Suitable for a quiet couple," suggesting the owners preferred no children. To make sure that "suggestion" came through, the ad simply declared, "No children or pets."

Home purchasing in the North State remained an option, with prices ranging from $3,200 to $4,250 within the city limits of Redding. The lower price was usually applied to a typical five-room small home located on a standard-sized lot of 50 by 180 feet. The owner asked for a "substantial" down payment while agreeing to take the balance as a "rent" payment of only $35 per month. Just outside of town, one would be able to acquire a home, usually on a one-acre lot, for the $4,250 noted above. One such home offered a detached large garage, a chicken house (fifty chickens included), five rooms in the main house and a fully irrigated acre of level land—a bargain compared to homes in the Sacramento environs or the Bay Area. Farther outside the city limits, such as in the mountains of Trinity County, one advertisement offered 160 acres, 18 of which were irrigated, a five-room house and four additional small cottages, each with two rooms, for a total sum of $20,000.

The fact remained clear as the war years progressed: housing would be difficult to find, especially anywhere near the Bay Area, and with rationed gasoline, it was difficult to impossible for home seekers to live in North State locations and commute to a war industry job in the Alameda or other Bay Area locations. Yet despite the obvious travel restrictions of gas rationing, North State residents saved enough coupons to take some time for short vacations to recreation sites in Northern California, including Scott's Ranch at the Trinity Center (Trinity County), Burney Falls, Hatchet Creek and Hat Creek.

CIGARETTES

Cigarettes remained a popular consumer product, and much money continually went into local newspapers' coffers for sponsoring leading tobacco brands. While many young men learned to smoke in the military, women also used tobacco regularly. In fact, during the war, with men overseas, women often appeared in large newspaper advertisements. In 1944, a major Camel cigarette ad featured Anne Bass, an inspector of navy binoculars for Universal Camera Company, agreeing with "the men in the service, who choose Camel as their favorite cigarette." With a broad, smiling face, posing in her work uniform, Bass is quoted saying, "Camels taste so Fresh....They're so easy on my Throat....They suit me to a 'Y.'" A graphic depiction of a female facing the camera is presented at the bottom of the ad with a *T* overlaid on her face, reaching from her throat area up and across her mouth; this diagram represented the "T-Zone" that made Camels the cigarette of choice.[55]

For much of the war, cigarettes appeared in the ration kits of American soldiers, freely and enthusiastically circulated and consumed. According to one report, "Soldiers were encouraged to smoke to relieve boredom and improve morale, and in 1943 their demand helped US companies manufacture 290 billion cigarettes." One interesting ad appeared in a magazine showing a young Ronald Reagan smoking a Chesterfield cigarette, with the caption, "I'm sending Chesterfields to all my friends. That's the merriest Christmas any smoker can have—Chesterfield mildness plus no unpleasant after-taste."[56]

EDUCATION

From the earliest weeks of World War II, elementary teachers introduced additional global geography into their lessons. Students learned that America now fought in two major theaters of war, Europe and the Pacific. From there, lesson activities included identifying the location of each country involved in the conflict and understanding which countries sided with the Allies, remained neutral or formed the Axis powers (Germany, Italy and Japan). In the middle grades, students researched in local newspapers to find the locations of current battles, the names of the generals leading U.S. forces and the progress of each conflict. Often, for science, teachers instructed students on topics related to weapons, their delivery and their explosive effectiveness; this, of course, became important in the last months of the war as the nation learned about the successful detonation of the atomic bomb. High school students during English class wrote extensively about their community's involvement in the war, who enlisted in which branch of service and communication between families and service members. High on the list of philosophy and writing, teachers asked students to analyze the differences between a democracy and Hitler's Germany, Mussolini's Italy or Hirohito's Japan, with a focus on appreciating the values traditionally celebrated in America.

Higher education, of course, saw a mass exodus of male students to the military. Many young women continued their post–high school education, and their enrollment increased as the war went on. Popular majors included business, education and mathematics. One North State woman, Ann Hunt, daughter of the then Shasta County superintendent of schools, Lucy Hunt, graduated among the top in her class at College of the Pacific, receiving special recognition awards and scholarships for achieving the highest grades in the graduating senior class. Ann, like her mother, decided to use the scholarship money to pay for her graduate courses in education, seeking to acquire a general secondary teaching credential. With summer free, Ann accepted a job as a camp counselor at Camp Minkalo in Amado County, sponsored by the Camp Fire Girls organization.

A teacher shortage in the North State did develop during World War II, with some late hires occurring after the start of the school year. Local newspapers placed advertisements for teacher openings and often listed teachers as they signed their contracts throughout the summers. Women assumed administrative and janitorial responsibilities as the war dragged on, something not seen prior to the war. Senior high school boys, sometimes as young as sixteen, who were tall for their age attempted at times to leave school and enlist. In fact, overall, high school enrollment declined from 6.7 million students nationwide in 1941 to 5.5 million in 1944. By that latter date, only one-third of the original teaching force was still earning their living in education.

Football remained a favorite sport for North State boys during the war; local authorities reasoned it provided physical training for possible future military service. Pictured above is the undefeated Chico High School football team, 1945. *Merriam Library Digital Collections.*

At Chico High School, a popular Cadet Corps program involved many boys in what was described as "learning by doing…a trend of many high school war-preparatory courses." Wearing cadet uniforms, these boys received special classroom training in the "winter months," then moved into field experiences with mock battles between companies of cadets. According to one source, a strict form of military discipline was mandated, with issuing orders coming from local military personnel volunteering their time and knowledge. Of the highest priority, teaching the eager cadets a sense of personal and group responsibility was emphasized throughout the training program. In addition to the Cadet Corps, Chico High boys actively engaged in all sports, particularly football, scoring an undefeated season in 1945.

One source noted that military officials involved with enlistments reacted in shock when they found out the lack of educational topics taught in the typical high school curriculum that were needed in the modern military. Of particular note, a high percentage of enlisted men could not read a map successfully, knowing little about orientation and almost nothing about map scales. Basic geometry also ranked low on the list of acquired skills from a high school education; this was related to all aspects of artillery delivery and bomb dropping. Within months, America's colleges reoriented their curricula to address some of the aforementioned topical issues, anticipating new jobs for those graduates skilled in specialized training and research; training focused on the expanding science fields, such as chemicals, plastics and metal alloys.

Colleges and universities such as Harvard made a full commitment to help the war effort in any way possible. James Conant, president of the university when America entered the war, stated, "The United States is at War....We are here tonight to testify that each one of us stands ready to do his part in ensuring that a speedy and complete victory is ours." Not only did the curriculum at the university undergo a transformation, but a close relationship also developed with the military, which effectively accepted, with priority, three thousand Harvard students, men and women, by the end of 1942. The provost, Paul Buck, made it clear to any candidate thinking that a Harvard acceptance meant anything but a total commitment to the war effort when he strongly declared, "College men need not be told again that they have no right to be in college unless they have planned their program in light of participation in the war." To this end, Harvard, and most educational institutions of higher learning, canceled summer vacations, establishing instead an additional teaching term of twelve weeks.[57]

Chapter 6

SHASTA DAM

What an opportunity, if Redding were ready to buy Shasta power,
to get our city known across the nation as the first to buy
and distribute cheap Central Valley power!
—America's Shasta Dam

Even before the Civil War ended, farmers in the Sacramento Valley clamored for more water. State water planners began drawing water source diagrams to assist local and regional water districts. As they realized their needs exceeded state resources, pressure mounted at the federal level for funds and technical engineering help. Nothing much came to the North State for decades, although the Army Corps of Engineers, along with the United States Reclamation Service, conducted more surveys of potential water sources and analyzed canal routes. However, with the disastrous beginning of the Great Depression and the need to use federal money to employ jobless men and women, the California state legislature passed the Central Valley Project in 1933, authorizing a bond promise totaling $170 million. North State leaders Judge Francis Carr and state senator John McColl traveled to Washington, D.C., hoping to convince the federal government to fund the state proposal. Given the already successful work on the monumental Boulder (later named Hoover) Dam, Congress voted to back the Central Valley Project, with plans to build two large dams, one in Northern California (Shasta) to harness the Sacramento River and one in central California (Friant) to hold back the rapid waters of the San Joaquin River. Plans called for the addition of canals, aqueducts, pumping stations, smaller dams and electrical transmission lines at a later date.

Getting Started

The Reclamation Service, recently renamed the United States Bureau of Reclamation, gained control of the bidding and construction plans for building the Shasta Dam. The final bid, won by a construction conglomerate, Pacific Constructors Incorporated (PCI), immediately hired Frank T. Crowe as superintendent of construction. Crowe, just finishing his masterful work on America's largest dam, Boulder, accepted the challenge.[58] By the summer of 1938, Crowe had convinced hundreds of men from his experienced workforce to follow him to Shasta County, the site selected for the large dam. After numerous investigations, Bureau of Reclamation engineers, under chief engineer Ralph Lowry, chose a location just south of where the McCloud and Pit Rivers flow into the Sacramento River, just a few miles north of the city of Redding. Here, steep canyon walls with solid rock foundations appeared the best geologic candidate for human transformation.

Before the first major stage of construction, excavation, could begin, Crowe and Lowry needed to build housing for an expected workforce numbering in the thousands. A threefold approach evolved as the announcement of expected job openings went out nationwide. First, the Bureau of Reclamation, desiring to segregate its inspection engineers, acquired land between Highway 99 and the building site, naming their little government town Toyon after the myriad of red berries growing in and around the area. Crowe preferred that his PCI engineers, foremen, managers and office personnel be housed at the dam site, just a few hundred yards downstream from the dam; the cluster of homes, offices, mess hall, recreation hall and supporting services took on the name Shasta Dam Village.[59] With national media coverage on the radio and in newspapers and magazines talking up the proposed size and duration of work on Shasta Dam, it was to be expected that many jobless families might check out Northern California. By September 1938, the number of men who had already arrived in Redding and around the job site swelled from a few hundred to somewhere over two to three thousand men, women and children, the adults hoping for any available work. The Redding branch of the United States Employment Service reported over 1,800 applications at this time.

Residents in Redding watched in amazement the unending flow of automobiles and people coming into town. The residents, themselves victims of the economic downturn, had little to offer in the way of immediate employment. Fraught with the ongoing stress of finding work, many families drove north and joined "tent camps" scattered on both sides of Highway 99,

Left to right: Frank Crowe, superintendent of construction for Pacific Constructors; Walker Young, construction engineer for the Bureau of Reclamation; and Ralph Lowry, chief engineer for the Bureau of Reclamation at Shasta Dam. All three men had worked together previously on Hoover Dam. *Bureau of Reclamation*.

The Bureau of Reclamation decided, as was its custom, to house its engineers and inspectors at a location separate from the immediate construction site and a short distance from the developing boomtowns. Offering three- and four-bedroom models, Toyon homes offered numerous amenities often lacking elsewhere, landscaping included. *Bureau of Reclamation.*

then along the two main roads heading to the job site. One observer, in late 1938, noted the "shock of the abject poverty and hopelessness, prevalent in the camps." Another noted the lack of sanitation and that "water had to be hauled in for miles, women, and babies gaunt-eyed and half-starved hoping and praying their husbands will get on at the dam."[60]

Accurate demographic characteristics are not available for the thousands of newcomers, but it is clear that the majority of them were men, mostly single men hoping to secure a job and begin a marketable construction career. Others, many others, were married men arriving with the last bit of their family's money, hoping to send regular payments home; some brought their families with them, understanding that they were part of Crowe's "construction family," moving on to the next big job, and so on and on—life in a construction camp. A few of the new arrivals simply came because it was California and it had to be better, economically, than their previous home in the East, South or Midwest.

NEW COMMUNITIES BUILT AROUND SHASTA DAM

With all the transportation action on the main east-to-west road going from Highway 99 to the dam site, bringing materials and people, it was only natural to expect that individual commercial stores and shops would open to serve the growing camp population. Slowly at first, with the explosion in commercial and residential activity from 1938 through 1941, the camps expanded into town-like communities, boasting names like Summit City, Project City and Boomtown (Central Valley). One of the first businesses to open, Polin's Little Reno, immediately found success offering locals, mostly men, games of pool, cards and snooker. Newspaper stands outside the main entrance offered the latest news on job openings and hiring schedules. J.C. Tibbitts, from nearby Redding, opened a Shasta Dam Information Center where newly arrived migrants might obtain information on housing and available land; he also sold real estate in the area that he had recently purchased in anticipation of incoming workers. He had nailed "BOOMTOWN" to a tall digger pine tree adjacent to his building. Soon service stations, grocery stores (later a Safeway), a theater (Shasta), restaurants, pool halls, drugstores and even a skating rink rose up in the environment of manzanita brush and digger pine trees. One of the largest early businesses, Phetteplace Variety Store, stocked many of the same dry goods found in larger Redding stores.

Small business establishments dotted the main road leading from Highway 99 to the dam site. Polin's Little Reno, a favorite drop-in store, arrived early on the dam building scene, offering a pool table and card playing, mostly for off-day single dam workers. *Bureau of Reclamation.*

Another early favorite stop-off for dam workers and their families was Wimpy's. Hamburgers and beer became a favorite, especially in the hot summer days of the first couple of construction years. Notice the large advertisement sign offering an "Air Cooled" environment inside. *Bureau of Reclamation.*

While the new boomtowns grew, work began on Shasta Dam. Excavation, diverting the railroad track and setting the forms commenced under the watchful eyes of Crowe and his team of dedicated supervisors and Lowry with his team of bureau inspectors. By December 7, 1941, the powerhouse and the primary dam foundation stood completed, with concrete slowly curing. Despite the fact that few Japanese Americans lived this far north in California, Lowry, working with the military command in San Francisco, ordered army guards to the site on hearing of the Pearl Harbor attack. Now, under strict surveillance, checkpoints for entry and exit from the dam site sprang up within a couple of days. Other associated sites, such as the nearby gravel-holding area and the conveyor belt bringing gravel from the Sacramento River site in Redding, saw twenty-four-hour patrols. The conveyor belt, the world's longest such system, ran ten miles over hilly terrain and appeared particularly vulnerable; if any section of the belt were destroyed, the entire delivery system would halt. Crowe and Lowry both understood this sobering fact, remaining vigilant and cooperative with local military authorities.

Eventually, the largest gathering of new homes and businesses coalesced along both sides of the road coming into the dam site from Highway 99, and this quickly growing community became known as Central Valley. The population grew from a few hundred in early 1938 to several thousand by the beginning of World War II. *Bureau of Reclamation.*

The Shasta Theater in Central Valley elevated the boomtown area, as patrons did not need to drive into Redding to see a motion picture. Seating 390 persons, the theater became an immediate success, especially with the installment of an air-conditioning system. *Bureau of Reclamation.*

In the boomtowns, everyone expected an air attack by Japanese carrier-based planes; rumors quickly spread that knocking out the dam would be a major victory for the enemy. Men working on the dam now needed to make a difficult decision: stay and work on Shasta Dam or quit and join the army or navy. Initially, patriotic workers leaned toward joining the fight, yet Crowe and Lowry tried to explain the importance of remaining on the job. Their main argument centered on the fact that in December 1941, the government wanted to finish the dam as quickly as possible, allowing transmission lines to connect vital war industries expanding in the Bay Area, especially the Kaiser Shipyards in the Alameda and Oakland area. From Crowe's standpoint, building the dam became the most patriotic choice a worker could make. Those men who stayed tried to keep focused on their work and families—remember, some of their families did not live in the Boomtown area but in other towns in California or in other states across the nation, and many families remained separated.

THE IMPORTANCE OF SHASTA DAM DURING WORLD WAR II

North State residents followed the early construction progress on Shasta Dam, as it offered reliable, ongoing employment for many left impoverished by the Great Depression. With the outbreak of war, military analysts and industrial companies quickly moved to ask the government to name the Shasta Dam project an A-1 defense priority, funneling monies to the site that might go elsewhere and preserving construction-material acquisition guarantees. John Page, U.S. Bureau of Reclamation commissioner, declared at the end of December 1941 that all efforts would be made to move the job along. The dam was already at 60 percent completion, and it was estimated that another three years would be needed to complete the concreting, the electrical power plant and the stringing of electrical wiring. Page made it known that for the time being, the focus remained on getting the power south. He wrote:

> *More electric power is needed in northern and central defense industries such as steel mills, magnesium, and chemical plants, oil refineries, shipyards, and automobile factories. Every effort is being made to speed up the construction of Shasta and Keswick Dams whose power plants will make available a total of 450,000 kilowatts of electric energy.*[61]

Despite the A-1 defense priority, dam workers became subject to the draft, with increasing public pressure to enlist. Bureau chief Lowry received approval to apply enlistment deferments to "key" personnel only; this meant highly skilled workers, managers, supervisors, inspectors and lead engineers.[62] A labor shortage did appear for a short time in 1942. To fill the gap of quitting workers, Crowe sent two buses down to Sacramento and the Bay Area, looking for anyone qualified in construction skills. However, well over half of the newly recruited workforce quit after realizing the dangerous nature of most jobs at the dam. To stop the continuing loss of men, Crowe authorized a significant pay raise; it did the trick. After a meeting, most workers agreed to stay on the job. Later, it was learned that many of them, mostly older men, already had plans to stay on in Shasta County, enjoying the beauty of the natural environment where California's great Central Valley meets the foothills of the Cascade Mountains—snow in the winter blanketing much of the area, yet gorgeous spring and fall weather, not too hot or too cold. Of course, they still needed to contend with the desperately hot summers.[63]

Black workers did find employment on Shasta Dam, but only in a limited capacity and in very low numbers, probably less than twenty persons. Hispanics, especially Mexicans, also worked at Shasta Dam; most of them were encouraged to leave their agriculture jobs as farm migrants and bused to the dam site. The Bureau of Reclamation successfully helped them move into the local labor union, assuring higher wages and benefits. It is assumed they lived in one of the three boomtowns, but government and civilian records do not disclose much information other than the fact that they appeared on the wage ledgers; their social experience when off work is not known.

As gasoline and tires became scarce under imposed rationing in the area, carpooling was encouraged, with the added benefit of allowing for closer, regular social contact between workers and families. "Neighbors came to depend on each other for hard to get [grocery] items and for seat space in automobiles." Local groups formed in each boomtown, with "a concerted effort to coordinate activities," carpooling remaining at the top of the list. Often, families rotated in turns to drive one or more persons from another family, with the destination usually Redding, for shopping or entertainment; one could save up their gas ration stamps for this purpose.[64]

Women Working at the
Shasta Dam Construction Site

As elsewhere in the North State, women in Shasta County, especially in the boomtowns, realized work opportunities abounded once World War II moved into mid-1942. Crowe and Lowry, where possible, tried to insert women employees into new job placements, including clerical, coffee shop, kitchen and mess hall positions. For example, Opal Foxx, a recent emigrant from Kansas, came to the dam site with the intent of visiting relatives. She immediately applied for work when rumors spread that a variety of current job openings existed at the much-visited coffee shop at Shasta Dam Village. A fast, efficient worker, Foxx next moved on to work in the main mess hall, serving hundreds of men coming and going from their work shifts on the dam. She started washing dishes for the swing shift at $3.20 for an eight-hour shift, reporting at six o'clock in the afternoon and working through until two o'clock the following morning. Continued success in this job resulted in her transfer to the day shift as a "relief cook." On her first day at the cooking ovens, one coworker explained that it was "bad luck" to have a female cooking in the kitchen. Brushing off the comments and veiled threats, Foxx exhibited her skills: turning, she grabbed a French carving knife and proceeded to fine-cut two crates of cabbage in "record time." Somewhat "amazed and bewildered, the male cooks, who had always used a large slicing machine to cut up cabbage, quickly accepted Foxx, and she remained on the job until the end of the war."[65] Later, with astonished fellow kitchen peers and some dam workers looking on, Foxx demonstrated how to crack eggs, one in each hand, at the same time, over and over again, filling the large black iron skillets.

Opal Foxx and others like her contributed a great deal to the war effort and local business. In many cases, their help kept the economic environment alive and well during the war. Vivian Jencks worked alongside her husband in keeping the ever-popular Donut Hole in Project City in the black, while June Murphy accepted a job as a cashier at Murphy's Grocery Store, another successful enterprise in Project City. At the same time, in the boomtown community of Central Valley, women worked at the local skating rink, Pike's Market and many other locations around the dam site. Meanwhile, in Redding, the local Office of Price Administration management hired dozens of women to help in a wide variety of clerical jobs, including managing the distribution of war coupons and coordinating and distributing government notices, rules and regulations.

Women, from the beginning of construction in 1938, worked in office environments at both the Bureau of Reclamation and Pacific Constructors Inc. sites at the dam. By the middle of 1942, other types of jobs opened as men left for military service; these included working in the kitchen, mail and parcel delivery and limited driving responsibilities. Note the navy recruitment poster. *Bureau of Reclamation.*

Like elsewhere in the North State, residents felt the impact of the war with the quickly rising prices of specific items. For example, the price of cheese, meat and coffee rose, almost immediately, by 20 percent, at times spiking to 30 percent. To offset these increased price hikes, Crowe and Lowry tried to raise wages at regular intervals. For those not working directly on the dam, wages averaged $0.99 an hour and rose to around $1.60 in 1945.

How the Dam Was Built

Throughout 1942, a complicated, well-choreographed system of dam construction moved along, and by March 28, 1942, the "3-Millionth Yard" of concrete rested in place, cooling in forms. Specialized engineers laid down miles of cooling pipes to assist the temperature reduction process, so necessary when placing large amounts of concrete.[66] The entire system of concrete placement, the most critical aspect of dam building, worked from a concept developed from the engineering genius of Crowe, conceived years earlier while working on a variety of smaller dams, then perfected on mighty Hoover Dam. A giant headtower, erected girder by girder from the bedrock of the Sacramento River, rose to the amazing height of 460 feet; its purpose entailed anchoring a unique series of strong, thick cables running from the headtower to several strategically placed tail towers located on the canyon walls. The tail towers ran on curved tracks, moving as needed to address different sections of the concrete placement. Running along the cables, eight-cubic-yard buckets rose up from the concrete pumping plant sitting immediately adjacent to the construction site. Once in the air, operators at the top of the headtower communicated with the tail tower operators to align their structures to line up the bucket over the next block of concrete forms.

Next, workers standing in the forms signaled when ready to have the bucket lowered; it was precision made possible by constant radio communication, learned hand signals and, of course, experience. Once the bucket arrived in the correct position, the bottom flaps of the bucket were released, dumping eight yards of freshly mixed concrete into the form. Now, the dirty work commenced. Workers spread the concrete and used powerful concrete vibrators to pack the material; one-man and two-man versions of the vibrators allowed for different applications of density packing. Meanwhile, the empty bucket, now making its way back to the concrete pumping plant, became available for another load. This construction sequence is, basically, how Shasta Dam rose upward from the Sacramento River bottom. Once

Frank Crowe, superintendent of construction, devised a unique system of concrete delivery, perfected over years of building dams in the American West. Using a series of coordinated towers and cables, the freshly mixed concrete moved from the mixing plant to specific block-forms, where waiting workers released the concrete and packed it into place. *Bureau of Reclamation.*

the system moved to a three-shift operation, rates of progress increased tremendously. Huge floodlights flashed on at dusk, illuminating the entire construction area, extending three-quarters of a mile across from one embankment to the other: impressive, yet slightly eerie. The idea of turning night into day on such a large scale seemed unbelievable; residents from as far away as Chico made the trip just to experience the scene.

Accidents, so prevalent during the construction of Hoover Dam, remained an ongoing concern at Shasta Dam. Safety rules, posted everywhere on the sprawling site, also appeared in the mess hall and recreation hall and on signs coming in and going out of the area. Crowe alerted all foremen to the responsibility incumbent on them to enforce all rules; violations became immediate grounds for job termination. Still, accidents occurred from the first weeks of road building and especially once the excavation began—dynamite charges being a prime culprit in the tunnel excavation when rerouting the train tracks. A job newsletter, the *Headtower*, distributed regularly to all workers posted new rules, reminded everyone of existing rules, listed recent accident incidents and even ran articles highlighting medical topics, such as heat exhaustion and necessary precautions. John Kirkpatrick, chief surgeon at the dam site, provided a quick and effective remedy for dealing with the unbelievably high summer heat. He advised workers to take "a tablespoon of Karo Syrup in a glassful of water before going to work, repeating at lunch and after arriving home."[67]

One issue of the *Headtower* with the headline "Accidents That Never Should Have Occurred" listed six recent episodes resulting in serious injuries and at least one fatality. It read,

1. *Electrician: one minute after going to work on swing shift, apparently lost his balance while walking along top of [concrete] form and fell 20 feet to his death. (Workmen are forbidden to walk along tops of forms. Use stairs and catwalks.)*
2. *Cement Pump Operator: caught finger in wheel of Fluxo pump, from which cover had been removed, and fractured finger severely.*
3. *Foreman: walking along top of fresh pour, caught foot in a wire, lacerating his leg.*
4. *Carpenter: hitting a bend, missed a rod and struck his foot, with a 10-pound hammer.*
5. *Blacksmith: grinding on an emery wheel, got particle of steel in his eye. NO GOGGLES!*
6. *Welder: grinding pump parts, had piece of steel hit his eye. NO GOGGLES.*[68]

On another occasion, a worker not wearing protective "innersoles" stepped on nails, with a loss of four workdays. Once a machinist helper, while working in a garage, "got an arc flash in both eyes," and was temporarily laid off, a loss of seven days; he wore no goggles. A newly hired laborer, working alongside his mentor, missed with a downward stroke of a sledgehammer, fracturing his partner's wrist; the injured worker lost three weeks in recovery. Apparently, the thousands of workers needed reminding about eye safety, so Crowe asked the newsletter editor to emphasize the issue. The editor wrote,

> *Your eyesight is a precious thing and there is no remedy for vision once destroyed. Nowhere are there spare parts to be procured to remedy your damaged vision. When this job is over, you men will probably have to pass a physical examination when you seek employment elsewhere and impaired vision is at the top of the list these days as a cause for rejection or employment. Goggles are available to every workman whose duties require him to work under circumstances where his eyesight is in jeopardy. We cannot stand over every man to enforce discipline, but we can do something about it if this flagrant disregard of our safety order about goggles is continued. The decision is up to you.*[69]

On the positive side, Crowe and Lowry regularly sponsored safety award events, recognizing workers achieving outstanding work records of no reported accidents.

Frank Crowe worked vigorously from the first days of excavation to set up and enforce safety procedures and protocols, but fatal accidents were bound to happen with thousands of men working in a confined area of steep slopes and temporary scaffolding; this was especially true of newly hired workers. One such accident occurred when a worker named William McCullough, hired only a week earlier, moved from his position on the concrete scaffolding to retrieve a wrench and take it to another location. He climbed down a ladder to a lower-level platform but "stepped through a hole in the [lower] platform" and fell sixty-four feet to his death, with "almost every bone in his body broken when he struck the concrete below."[70]

Work on the dam in 1942 included laying down the first sections of the gigantic fifteen-foot-long penstocks, sporting diameters wide enough to drive a school bus through; the job of the penstocks centered on funneling water from the soon-to-be reservoir to the powerful turbine engines in the

The tall structure is the headtower from which all concrete delivery cables emanated. On the lower left, the powerhouse sits, as the water-delivery penstocks are shown projecting from the dam downward, where they will eventually connect to the turbines, thus generating electrical power. The dam itself is rising as each block of concrete is placed; note the Sacramento River still flowing in the center of the dam site, later to be diverted through a side diversion tunnel. *Bureau of Reclamation.*

powerhouse. Super large X-ray machines scanned each joint of the newly welded penstock sections, ensuring no leaks. At the same time, Lowry, informed by the local Wintu tribe that the Curl Cemetery, a traditional burial site, might be flooded when the reservoir filled, ordered a special team of men to work with the Indians to relocate the bodies.

In August 1942, workers celebrated placing the four millionth yard of concrete, and the dam looked well on its way to completion. Meanwhile, in the boomtowns, off-duty men talked war news: anything to keep the conversation off their work on the dam. Women, like elsewhere in small towns of the North State, formed sewing clubs, mending old and new garments that might be used in the war effort. Children, with their mothers, constantly held recycling drives, looking for tin, rubber, glass and specific metal scraps.

COMPLETING SHASTA DAM

As a new year, 1943, began, Crowe and Lowry received briefings from visiting Bureau of Reclamation officials, recently arrived from Washington, D.C., on the need to bring one or two of the power generators online as soon as possible. Workers dropped the massive scroll cases for Stations 1 and 2 turbines in January; the turbines would come later. Striking out from the dam and heading south, workers began laying out the heavy-duty cable wires destined to transfer the electrical energy from the dam site to locations in the Bay Area. Later in the year, top government officials decided to reroute two incoming turbines to Grand Coulee Dam in Washington; no explanation was given at the time, other than that the decision was made at the "highest levels" as a war priority.[71]

Later, as the weather warmed in June, burly bulldozers broke open the upstream dirt-packed cofferdam; the cofferdam, designed to funnel river water, channeling it through an area known as Block No. 40, had also successfully held back Sacramento River water from entering the river diversion tunnel. Now water gushed through the tunnel, emerging downstream of the dam construction. With the water diverted from the drying riverbed, work on the remaining center block, Block No. 40, of the dam could begin, placing concrete in ever-rising tiers.

It was a big day in July 1944 when Bureau of Reclamation officials notified local authorities that the hydroelectric power plant stood complete and ready to produce electricity. While federal authorities made it perfectly clear that electrical priority rested on supplying energy to the Bay Area's wartime production plants, including the Kaiser Shipyards, local citizens hoped that some of that electricity might come to them. One North State resident, living in Redding, stated what everyone else was thinking: "What an opportunity, if Redding were ready to buy Shasta power, to get our city known across the nation as the first to buy and distribute cheap Central Valley power!"[72]

By the end of 1944, Shasta Lake water levels were rising quickly; local residents and others in nearby counties took notice, thinking of the possible recreational benefits and considering future business opportunities all along the proposed extensive shoreline. Already, despite gas rationing, some families drove to the Pit River Bridge, where easy access to the lake existed, dragging their small sailboats and motorboats, hoping for an afternoon of lake cruising. On any given weekend, "attractive girls in bathing suits, skimming across the surface of the lake on surf-boats behind fast boats" became a regular occurrence. Of course, gas rationing did limit this activity for the time being, but local officials saw postwar lake recreation as a huge economic boon to the North State. Fishing on the lake, just getting started in 1944, looked like a strong incentive to lure locals and out-of-the-area enthusiasts to the lake.

One way to visit the lake involved answering one of the many ride-sharing ads in local newspapers. Ride-sharing complemented gas rationing as a logical way to save fuel. The Office of Defense Transportation (ODT) set up regional departments to help coordinate local war transportation committees. Tom L. Stanley chaired Shasta County's committee. These officials first talked with commercial truckers to work out burgeoning concerns over a lack of truck replacement parts and tires and gasoline shortages. A "Share the Ride" program soon developed, asking store employees to fill out information cards detailing their place of residence and working hours. The thrust of the effort looked to coordinate commuters living outside town limits in a system of geographic ridesharing and then expanded to help those requesting rides for recreation or family and friend visits in other parts of the North State. Shasta Dam remained a top destination for North State residents looking for something new to do, wanting to see for themselves the sheer size of the construction site and worker activity.

The final bucket of concrete placement occurred on December 22, 1944, amid picture-taking celebrations throughout the day. Little did the gathered leaders—Frank Crowe and company, engineers, foremen, administrators and other workers—know that Shasta Dam would be the last large concrete dam built in America. Hundreds of dam workers made the decision to remain in Shasta County; interviews with over one hundred of them revealed to this author their strong desire to finally settle down in the beautiful surroundings of Northern California.[73] Additionally, they realized that their specialized skills, honed to perfection while working on the dam, opened expected job opportunities in a postwar economy; and they were right.

Interestingly, Frank Crowe received, on the night of May 22, 1945, a phone call from the War Department. He was home at that time, in his large two-storied house perched at the top of Placer Street in Redding, overlooking the city, the river and the Cascade Mountain Range. The caller, an army general, wanted to propose a job opportunity. During the call, Crowe became aware that political and military officials needed to coordinate the rebuilding of war-torn Germany, recently surrendered and having suffered devastating destruction to its infrastructure by round-the-clock bombing by the Allies. Factories, rail lines, roads, airports, numerous public buildings and dams—yes, dams—needed repair or, in many cases, a complete reconstruction.[74] The offer included overall construction authority as engineer-in-charge for rebuilding projects in the soon-to-be American Zone, located in the western portion of Germany.[75] Honored by the recognition, Crowe and his wife considered the offer, eventually turning it down. Frank, sixty-two years old at the time, wanted to live at his home in Redding, relax at his newly acquired sprawling cattle ranch in the foothills of the Cascades and take on, from time to time, construction offers to his liking. However, sadly, he did not have long to live; he suffered a fatal heart attack on February 26, 1946. Recognitions from hundreds of political and industrial leaders poured in from around the country in the next few days, confirming what many North State residents already knew: Frank Crowe was America's master dam builder.

Chapter 7

NORTH STATE MEN AND WOMEN
IN THE MILITARY

P atriotic fervor exploded in America after the bombing of Pearl Harbor, and men eighteen years old and older rushed to enlist. One interesting phenomenon of this ongoing event saw newly enlisted men eagerly seeking marriage engagements with high school sweethearts. In Butte County, recorded marriages doubled from 117 in 1940 to 242 during 1942. According to one article in a local newspaper, men leaving for the service apparently wanted to be sure that their sweethearts would be waiting for them on their return; this was an important factor in the minds of most young men.

EAGER TO SERVE

Even before Pearl Harbor, North State youths signed up to serve in the military. William Johnson, from the little town of Biggs, participated in a top-secret mission in the Army Air Corps in September—before Pearl Harbor. The excited twenty-two-year-old, unaware of his final destination, eagerly boarded his B-17G Flying Fortress somewhere in the Bay Area for a flight to Oahu, Hawaii. In December 1941, just a couple of weeks after Pearl Harbor, the government revealed a summary report of the flight. The *Gridley Herald* picked up the story, declaring, "Biggs Youth One of 72 to Receive Flying Cross" and then describing a "secret mass flight" from Honolulu to the Philippines in which Johnson participated. Johnson's parents received notice that their son had received recognition for his "heroism and extraordinary achievement"; no details were revealed. Not until recently has the full story been known of Johnson's flight.

Military officials in Washington recognized the need for more bomber aircraft to help defend the Philippines should war begin with Japan. To this end, the mission received the go-ahead. While Royal Australian Air Force (RAAF) flights of purchased American Catalina aircraft had flown the "Pacific Route" to New Zealand and Australia, no American B-17s had done so; Johnson's flight would be the first. The first leg from Hawaii involved a 2,400-mile flight to Wake Island, then a night leg to Port Moresby, entailing flying fourteen hours, part of it over the Japanese-claimed Caroline Islands. One source noted this leg of the journey forced the pilots not to use their running lights, cruising at an altitude of twenty-five thousand feet, close to their recommended ceiling height. The newspaper account did not identify Johnson's job on his plane, but the airplanes did maintain radio silence during this nerve-wracking portion of the flight, landing safely on September 8, 1941. The final run of the journey took the planes to Clark Field at Darwin, Australia, where mechanics serviced the planes; later, the army sent them north to the Philippines. The December news account claimed these planes "have been [since] heavily engaged in defense of the islands [Philippines]."[76] One can imagine Johnson's state of mind on this mission. The flyer knew that his time had come to serve. His long hours of daily training predicted his next course of action, fighting the Japanese in and around the Philippines.

North State men and women served in many capacities during World War II. Several Shasta County youths were among the first to join the marines in 1942. They were William Crumpacker of Redding, Walter Armstrong from Cottonwood and Robert Corella of Central Valley. Having passed their medical examinations and interviews, the three new marines left for induction in San Francisco on January 21, 1942.

In early 1943, William Dax, from the Gridley area, learned aviation mechanics at Sheppard Field, Texas, with the goal of keeping bombers and fighter aircraft in serviceable condition. With his advanced training, he set the goal of becoming a crew chief, hoping to work on the maintenance of bombers exclusively. Along with his promotion to crew chief, he wrote home expressing his additional hope of achieving the rank of corporal or sergeant. Other Gridley young men found assignments "somewhere in North Africa" or "somewhere in the South Pacific"; government regulations clearly forbid soldiers writing letters home from designating specific geographical areas that might shed light on individual army or navy units in each theater of war.

Private George Murphy, serving in the Army Air Corps, trained in Sacramento, Fresno and St. Louis. Murphy learned of his first overseas station: India, where he was to assist Allied efforts to regain the initiative in Southeast Asia. The Japanese had successfully invaded and defeated forces in the Malaya Peninsula, and moving on, they captured British-controlled Singapore. As the summer of 1942 approached, the Japanese were poised to strike at India, having subjugated much of Southeast Asia. Murphy's contribution, though his specific job is unknown, helped deter further Japanese aggression in the Indian Ocean region. Interestingly, George's brother, Elzy, was destined to fight in the European continent. He landed with American troops during the Anzio invasion of Italy in January 1944, received wounds and was transferred to a hospital in Auburn, not far from his North State home.

Corporal Byron Ball from Oroville, serving in a tank battalion in central Italy, received a letter from an Oroville resident that he did not know, Mrs. Mario Zaccanti. The recently arrived American immigrant, Mrs. Zaccanti, had read that Ball's unit had been fighting for five hundred days, moving sluggishly up the Apennine Mountains in central Italy, where her family still lived. She asked Ball if he could "learn the whereabouts [of her family] should he pass through the little village where they have their home." When Ball's reply arrived in April 1945, Zaccanti was happy to find that her mother, in her eighties, was "weakened by sacrifices of war" but still in good general health. Zaccanti's brother-in-law, however, had recently died when a bomb exploded in the village. In his letter, Ball described the "great joy" expressed by the Italian people on their liberation and the "kindness of the natives to American soldiers and the beauty of the Italian countryside in the spring."[77]

WOMEN IN THE MILITARY

Women, too, served in the military. Norene McAfee worked diligently for the Shasta County Clerk's Office in Redding before joining the Women Accepted for Volunteer Emergency Service (WAVES), sometimes known as the Women's Reserve. McAfee held the same last name as the first director of the WAVES, Mildred McAfee, but was afforded no special treatment during her training at Hunter College in New York City; all enlisted women trained at this one location, beginning in 1943. Norene wrote home regularly to keep her family informed of her progress. It is interesting to note that much controversy surrounded the initiation of the women's reserve unit. Little support came from Congress or the navy, but constant pressing by influential women, such as Eleanor Roosevelt, on the Navy Women's Advisory Council—and of course, Eleanor's direct line to her husband, the president—helped to promote the organization.

Another WAVES graduate, Corinne Claire Yetter, spent the early part of the war at Stanford University, graduating with honors. Immediately after graduation, she returned home to her parents in Redding for a short time. There, in discussions with her parents and local authorities, she determined to join the WAVES, leaving the North State in the late summer of 1944 for training at the administrative center at Hunter College.

Local North State young women also volunteered to join the Women's Army Corps (WACS). The original name of the organization, begun in mid-1942, was the Women's Auxiliary Army Corps (WAAC), later changed to WACS. Women joining the WACS received full pay and benefits as men; this helped bring in 150,000 women to the noncombat organization. The slogan ran, "Free a man for combat" by working jobs such as weather observer, office worker or administrator, teacher or driver. Leona Erhardt, of Shasta County, ably filled the latter position. A former teacher, Erhardt went off to basic training, then was sent to special training for her eventual assignment as an assistant and staff car driver for the war department at Fort Myer, Virginia.

By 1944, the demand for women nurses had increased dramatically, particularly for service in the navy. The Navy Nurse Corps, two days after D-Day, called for an immediate drive to induct more women. The offer looked inviting, including recognized professional medical standing and a fully authorized commission as an officer in the navy. The opportunities existed for the current call to serve overseas in base hospitals now being planned for France and the western Pacific. Other areas of service existed on hospital ships and in the Hospital Corps Training Schools, located in various bases around the nation. Qualifications required the applicant to hold a registered nurse's diploma and be between the ages of twenty-one and forty, single and in good health. The nearest recruitment office for North State women was located in San Francisco.[78]

NORTH STATE MEN IN COMBAT

Combat stories circulated throughout North State communities as news of homegrown soldiers' participation and heroics appeared in newspapers and during general conversations around town. The D-Day invasion and subsequent battles in France and Belgium placed North State young men in difficult, stressful combat situations, calling for extraordinary effort. One such extra effort saw Robert Jex of Redding of the Ninth Air Force Command awarded the Air Medal, given for "heroic or meritorious achievement while participating in aerial flight." Given orders to fly over the heavily defended skies of western Germany, Jex, in an aerial gunner on a twin-engine Douglas A-20 Havoc medium bomber, kept enemy fighters at bay, allowing the bomber group to continue its assignment. The bomber group's commander, Colonel Ralph Rhudy, recommended Jex for the medal with the special understanding that his men had been asked to continue "round-the-clock" missions behind enemy lines, bombing key German military targets. Just a regular kid, Jex graduated from Shasta Union High School and was employed as a salesclerk when the war broke out. Like many of his male classmates, Jex enlisted in January 1942.

In the Pacific, American forces struggled to gain the offensive against early Japanese successes in the Philippines, Southeast Asia and the islands of the South Pacific. James Riggins of Anderson, California, saw action in New Guinea and "other islands of the Pacific." Riggins, along with other local North State young men, joined the local National Guard unit in 1941 and later assimilated into Company F of the 115th Combat Engineers. Along with a letter to his father in 1944, Riggins sent home Japanese souvenirs, including a rising sun flag autographed by him and his two buddies, Sergeant Elmer Bidwell and Sergeant Art Hoyer. His father displayed the flag with other "souvenirs" for curious local residents to see; these items included a captured "long barrel 25-caliber rifle, a Japanese soldier's wallet, containing money and photos—one smeared with blood, a waist money belt, and a cigarette case."[79]

Worry over North State sons and husbands fighting in the Philippines stressed residents, as news during the early months of the war proved depressing, with Japanese forces scoring a string of victories deploying overwhelming forces. The parents of Grover Knox, of Red Bluff, finally received a war department notice that their son had been wounded "in action." The cablegram noted the date of December 22, 1941, as the day Grover received his wound, but no further information came forward as the days dragged on. Friends and local authorities suggested that the young man, along with thousands of others, had been evacuated to Australia, reviving hope that Grover was not a prisoner of war. War news depressed the Knoxes more as Japanese troops pushed Americans onto a small peninsula, Bataan, with heavy casualties incurred on both sides and rumors spreading in America of cruel treatment of captured prisoners, wounded or not. One group of entrepreneurs in Oroville met to discuss the impact of war rationing on their business, citing tires and gas as the main culprits limiting profits, but the discussion quickly moved to the deteriorating military situation in the Philippines and the hopelessness of General MacArthur's forces.[80]

War Department notices and cablegrams communicated reported casualties to anxious parents. Not knowing, at any one time, where their sons were fighting, North State mothers and fathers tried to follow the movements and actions of major military units and their participation in combat situations. Private Edmund Cross, native to the small hillside community of Buckeye, was first reported missing in action after the fall of Corregidor in the Philippines in 1942. Cross's mother, like many other wartime parents, did not receive any further communication until sometime later—in this case, in the summer of 1944, when the War Department officially changed his designation to "lost in action." Young Cross had moved with his family to the East Bay and graduated from a Richmond high school. From there, he went on to join the Army Air Corps in 1940, serving as an aircraft mechanic at various military stations in California and New Mexico before receiving orders to proceed to the Philippines. Along with the 1944 notification, Cross's mother received, for her son, a Purple Heart, a posthumous reward in recognition of Edmund's service.

In the middle of the war, news, good and bad, flooded newspaper front pages, worrying family members as each new battle was announced. Letters home to parents expressed different opinions of military service and experiences. Richard Keener of Oroville, last reported to be on the destroyer USS *Waller*, was believed by his parents to be somewhere in the southwest Pacific. His parents gave details: Richard said that "the navy is great and that he loves his ship, a new destroyer.…[The ship] never rides the waves but cuts right through them as it is plenty fast." The elder Keeners were relieved to find out that their son, riding out severe storms, never became seasick. A little homesick, though, Richard claimed he had seen "a lot of foreign places," but Oroville was still "the best." The young Keener proudly reported his rapid rise in rank and responsibility, now serving as seaman 1C on a torpedo crew; in short order, he expected to rise to the rank of petty officer. A graduate of Oroville High School, the young man entered the service in June 1942, enlisting for six years, and left for overseas in January 1943. As a military graduate of the Torpedo School at the base in San Diego, Keener received a final ranking score of 19.27 percent, one of the top honor students in his class.[81]

From the little town of Palermo, Mr. and Mrs. David Shaw let the local newspaper know that their son, David Jr., had written home from Kingman,

Arizona, to announce his promotion to the rank of sergeant. The young Shaw initially joined the service on June 3, 1941, before Pearl Harbor, first training at Sacramento's Mather Field and later receiving special training at various bases on the West Coast and in the East. In Arizona, Shaw worked diligently, learning the stressful job of head and tail gunner on B-17 and B-24 Liberator aircrafts. Before entering the military, Shaw worked the Oroville gold dredge and received career welding training in Chico.

First Lieutenant Ernest Carey, of Gridley, received special recognition while serving as copilot in bombing runs over Wake Island in the Pacific. He was credited with bravery by his plane commander, William Matheny, for helping drop seventy-six thousand pounds of explosives on Japanese positions at key locations on Wake Island. His parents, in a local newspaper article, explained the intensive training their son received before he was ordered out to the Pacific theater of operations, first going to Stockton, followed by stations at Pendleton, Oregon; Spokane, Washington; a Texas airfield; and finally Sioux City, Iowa.[82] A later newspaper article on Carey noted that the brave young man was now in Hawaii receiving his decoration for distinguished service.

Another Gridley soldier wrote home describing his recent deployment in Africa:

> *Dear George:*
>
> *Well, here I am way over here in Africa and going strong. But there's no country like the good old USA. We sure have plenty to fight for. Coming over on the boat I was pretty seasick for the first couple of days out. But got my sea legs and [I] am a pretty good sailor. We landed and took our objective, and I came through without a scratch, altho [although] some of them came pretty close.*
>
> *The natives here are sure primitive. They do their plowing with a wooden plow drawn by a camel and donkey. Not many cars here. And what there are burn coal instead of gas. The natives dress like they did in Biblical days, just a robe thrown around them. I've gotten your paper twice now and it sure picks a guy up.*[83]

A penetrating look at war from one North State veteran provided local readers with an in-depth account of combat battle for the first time. The soldier, writing from "somewhere in the Marshalls," described his experience during action in the Marshall Islands campaign, writing,

I was in the Marshall Island deal, and it was some battle. I'm still wondering how I got out without a scratch. We were in the front lines three days and three nights. The battle was over just about as fast as it started. I got a slug [bullet] through my pack [backpack]. I was shaky the first time I tried to shoot a [enemy soldier] and missed: after that it came easy and right now I have accounted for five that I know of but have no idea as to how many I got with hand grenades. It's kinda funny about those guys. I thought I would kinda hate to shoot one, but I didn't. I got a lot more kick out of shooting ducks when at home. The only thing here is they shoot back at you. They aren't as tough as I thought and once you get them cornered all you have to do is use a few grenades.[84]

Each North State serviceman and woman looked forward to official leave or furlough, returning home to family and friends. The length of granted time varied considerably, as did the reasons for the time away. Mid-1943 was a particularly stressful time as America attempted to take the offensive in both the European and Pacific theaters of war, planning this month for the invasion of Italy, one of the Axis powers and an enemy of America at that time. Sometimes the visits home involved days or just a few hours, with service members coming in on a train and leaving that evening. This was the case with Second Lieutenant Oscar Hermann. Having just completed his training at the Army Air Corps Instrument School at Bryan Field in Texas, the officer came home to Oroville, gaining a few days for a leave before his new post at Air Corps Advanced Flying School, Luke Field, Arizona, where he would serve as a top-rated flying instructor. Learning that his parents now lived in the Bay Area, Hermann, once home, asked to visit his friends in the Oroville area. Fortunately, his parents had saved enough gas stamps to motor, by car, to Oroville. Visits home helped give combat-bound soldiers and sailors a feeling of relaxation, connectedness and purpose that provided, for a brief but precious time, a psychological break from intense training and the anxious feelings of combat anticipation.

As stated earlier, one of the highlights for a service member, whether overseas or somewhere outside the North State, included receiving one or more copies of local newspapers. Private Lawrence Johnson, a marine, formerly of Gridley and the Biggs area and now serving somewhere in the South Pacific, wanted to show his appreciation for a newspaper sent from the Gridley General Hospital. The letter read,

I wish to express my gratitude for your kindness in sending me your paper. It's a great morale builder and helps me to keep up with the daily home news. We Marines overseas in the South Pacific really appreciate each little bit of news we receive from home and eagerly await the mail-calls which are few and far between. To you and all of my friends at home, I wish to send my "Season's Greetings" and hello![85]

For those North State service members stationed in the Midwest or the East, finding transportation to California proved difficult and, often, uncomfortable. Take the case of William Henderson of Oroville. Granted a fifteen-day furlough from his base in Camp Forrest in Tennessee, Henderson reported to the train station to find every seat filled. In fact, the seating car itself was filled with standing soldiers and civilians. Forced to wait for the next train or stand on the boarding steps, he chose the latter, standing all the way from Tullahoma, Tennessee, to Kansas City, Missouri, a distance of four hundred miles. From Kansas City, he moved into a seat as detraining passengers left; he tried not to leave his seat for the rest of the trip to California.

By 1944, rules restricted draft men from being granted leave once they reported to their reception or induction center. Leonard Hill of Gridley and four others reported to the Fort Ord reception center at Monterey with the idea that once their preliminary paperwork was concluded and approved, they would have time to return home for a brief goodbye and to settle any outstanding affairs. Hill, once he found out about the new rule, asked for permission to return for a short time, as a special case, to clean up business dealings, only to have his request denied. Hill had this confirmed by the chairperson of the local draft board; it seems communication on the new rule did not reach new draftees.

North State Families Learn the Fate of Serving Military Personnel

The year 1944 saw numerous letters finally coming to North State parents and wives concerning the family service member, including those known to be prisoners of war. Gene Wooten, of Marysville, became a prisoner of the Japanese at the surrender at Corregidor. Wooten's short letter provided a thankful break from their constant worry about their son's condition, especially since rumors of Japanese atrocities against American prisoners circulated frequently, some with merit. In March that year, he wrote, "We have musical instruments in camp and hold amateur contests on Sundays and holidays. So, I haven't forgotten how to play a guitar. Tell Frank [his brother] we have a hillbilly band that is really good. In my spare time, I am studying the Japanese language."[86]

Meanwhile, from Europe, H.A. McLoughlin of Yuba City received his first letter from his son, Pat, a technical sergeant, who was captured by German troops and sent to a prisoner of war camp whose location was unknown to Pat. He wrote, "Dear Dad: I was shot down October 8 [1943], slightly wounded, but have fully recovered. We are treated well, and I feel fine. All of us have had our hair, cut clipper short. Dad, contact the Red Cross to see how and what you can send me."[87]

The North State Reacts to D-Day

By mid-1944, everyone knew that the massive buildup of Allied forces in England stood ready, poised to invade Europe and liberate Nazi-occupied territory; everyone knew it, and everyone prayed. In the Marysville–Yuba City area, the local newspaper placed a proclamation on the front page. It read,

> *To folks of all faiths the mayors of Marysville and Yuba City today addressed a proclamation calling for work and prayer for the victory that is presaged by the Allied invasion of Europe. Churches throughout the community meanwhile opened their doors to those who would join in the prayer for a quick liberation [of] nations enslaved by the Nazis and a prompt victory for [the] Allies' army over the German enemy. "Let their [sic] be devotion in the community today and henceforth to the certainty of victory and for the success of our arms in this hour of climax," said the proclamation signed by Mayor Alvin Divver of Marysville and Mayor S.J. Flanery of Yuba City. "Let us join with the Allied world in prayer, not only in our homes but in the places of worship in the community, that our united voice may be heard by the Universal Judge in support of the brave boys who are carrying our cause over distant battlefields."[88]*

As with Pearl Harbor, North State residents listened intently, anxiously, as news dribbled describing the landings at the Normandy beaches. It was Tuesday, a workday, yet it remained the topic of conversation in work and leisure environments; everyone wanted to know if the invasion had successfully secured the beaches. Allied leaders, such as Prime Minister Winston Churchill, wanting to reassure the American public, announced that by the evening of June 6, Allied forces had "smashed their way inland on a broad front." This comment later proved to be a bit optimistic, and British, American, Canadian and other Allied units met fierce resistance in some areas. Churchill did admit, "Heavy fighting will soon begin and will continue. It is therefore a most serious time that we are entering upon."[89]

On June 6, Pacific Telephone and Telegraph Company, in recognition of the increasing demand for communication supplies to support the European invasion, let the North State know that no new telephone equipment or repair supplies would be available to civilians. The notice made it clear,

> *There's no more new equipment now. The Army and Navy have first call on that....As we scrape the bottom of the barrel, we're trying hard to make what we have do the best possible job by—*
> *Stretching switchboards to make room for more lines and calls.*
> *Making former one-party lines serve two or more families wherever possible and necessary.*
> *Reconditioning all serviceable facilities and putting them to use.*

The notice brought home the valid, though concerning, point that no one should complain about the current situation, reminding readers, "Nobody likes to stand in line. But it's different when the line forms behind our fighting men."[90]

The next day, June 7, newspapers throughout the North State carried the news that the fifth war loan drive would begin the following week. Timing for this release coincided with the desire to support the European invasion: "As the tempo of invasion rises, every one of us must mobilize for support of our fighting men." The government stated a bond drive goal of $16 billion, with $6 billion coming from individuals. The loan program offered several investment opportunities, including Series E, F and G savings bonds; Series C savings notes; 2.5 percent bonds of 1965–70; and 1.25 percent notes, Series B of 1947. The theme for the drive became "Back the Attack—Buy More Than Before."

A June 7 editorial titled "The Final, Fateful Step" summed up the feeling of just about everyone in the North State, starting with these words: "We are set for the final rounds, thank God!" The pent-up frustration of waiting for the moment to strike with an overwhelming force now burst forth as people understood that D-Day was, hopefully, the beginning of the end. However, the editor made it clear that "this is not [a] subject for loud rejoicing; so much as it is for sobering contemplation, unremitting labor, and prayer for the desired end." In a powerfully moving sentence, the reader learned that a "successful conclusion of the fight cannot come too soon to please the great mass of Americans whose lifeblood is at stake in the battle and whose homes have been shorn of their flower to supply the fiendish appetites of war."[91]

In Oroville, all churches opened their doors for worship despite D-Day being a Tuesday, encouraging all residents to feel free to come in and pray throughout the day and evening. Special services offered specific prayers and music to help citizens participate in the company of their community peers. Individual and private family prayer opportunities remained available for days following the initial landing, as news of the enormous invasion captured the attention of the nation, particularly families with husbands or sons known to be in Europe at that time. With headlines reading, "Allies Invade France and Fliers View Huge Armada Invasion," the odds increased that North State soldiers would be part of the evolving epic confrontation.[92]

Positive reports permeated the initial news coming from military sources and local government officials. One local paper assured Butte County citizens, "As for the success of the invasion, it is not doubted. Germany is hemmed in from all sides. She is tired. She has lost control of the air and is weak on the sea." On the same day, a local business in Oroville reminded everyone of who these soldiers were that assaulted the Normandy beaches: "His name is Smith, Kelly, Wilson, Levin, Olson. He comes from Oroville, Woodland, Chico, Palermo, Quincy, and Greenville. He is bigger than anything that can happen to him. He is a farmer, mechanic, lawyer, miner, stockman, woodsman, and cop. He is body and soul, not an identification tag."

Within two days, the full story of the tragedy and success was coming out in local papers. One headline ran, "We Land in France," with a subheading, "4000 Ships, 11,000 Planes Take Fighting Men to Whip the Nazis." On this same day, one Oroville family learned the fate of its service members serving on the escort carrier USS *Block Island*. Their three sons, Clyde, Jack and Gordon Cannon, served together on the same ship. The carrier, on a combat station near the Canary Islands in May 1944, became victim to the German U-boat *U-549*. The enemy U-boat cleverly eluded the destroyer screen surrounding the *Block Island*. Thankfully, though the carrier took at least two torpedo hits, most of the ship's 957 crew made it safely off the ship, including Clyde, Jack and Gordon. However, the Abeck family, also from Oroville, also had a son serving on the carrier, and as of December

8, 1944, they had not yet heard the fate of their son, Nick.[93] Events such as this represent the elation and depression endured by North State families throughout World War II.

Daily news of the June 6 D-Day invasion brought special attention to North State residents, who knew some of their sons participated in the beach assaults. Knowing this, conscientious service members taking part in the invasion tried their best to write home. Weeks later, one North State serviceman, James Hoffstot, did write home describing his actions as a Navy Seabee in the days following the initial landings.

> *We worked for 94 hours without relief and with from one to two hours sleep early each morning, when the gun-fire was at its worst. It is quiet around here now, almost peaceful. I am feeling fine, just a little sleepy.*[94]

Hoffstot's parents in Redding shared the letter openly, suggesting their son's activity as a Seabee probably centered on unloading and organizing the huge amount of equipment and supplies, "on the beaches," that combat troops continually needed as the units proceeded inland through the French countryside. The letter goes on to allude to the fact that Hoffstot attempted to make contact and carry on conversations with French civilians in and around the area, apparently handing out cigars as an incentive to show friendship. The young Seabee had graduated from the local high school only one year prior to the D-Day landing.

First Lieutenant George Backes of Central Valley served in the Army Air Corps, seeing extended service in Europe. Assigned to a B-26 Marauder—a twin-engine medium bomber that, at first, carried the ominous nickname *Widowmaker*[95]—Backes overcame challenges and survived numerous missions over German targets at a time when early models of the plane regularly incurred serious takeoff and landing problems. By mid-1944, Backes had achieved a monumental step, completing his fiftieth mission as a pilot. The crew nicknamed their plane *Dina Might*, thankful for their good luck. Backes, for his part, received the Distinguished Flying Cross, the Air Medal with eight oak leaf clusters, one bronze cluster and one silver cluster.

Another young man, this one from Redding, worked behind the lines at a British airfield to recondition, as quickly as possible, Allied bombers and fighters, British and American, so "they may rise again against the enemy." Verne Sayre, who had grown up in the North State and volunteered for active duty in October 1942, received his basic training in Florida; then he traveled to Lowry Field in Colorado for more in-depth training. Next, orders declared that he needed more training at Clovis Air Base in New Mexico and then at the Tucson Army Air Base in Arizona. Finally, he received his overseas assignment in December 1943. The above list of training bases gives the reader some idea of the constant and varied training experience aircraft mechanics received during World War II; their role was vital in helping the American military secure and maintain air superiority in the skies over Europe and the Pacific.

As the American army worked to break out of the D-Day beaches, progress in Italy slowed. In 1943, Allied armies invaded Sicily and quickly moved on to a planned invasion of Italy. However, bogged down in Italy, after the Anzio invasion of 1943, Allied progress slowed as German forces reinforced their lines, literally digging in a strong defense. As American progress slowed, soldiers spent idle time writing home from their foxholes and trench positions. Such was the case with Private Paul McDermott. The young man, only a junior at a North State High School, entered the service as a talented artist and musician. Along the way, he penned a letter to his parents; he appropriately titled his letter, "Foxhole Thoughts," pouring out his feelings about growing up and wondering about a philosophy of life, death and God. He wrote,

> *We are born struggling little mortals....We are thrilled at the stimulating aspect of life. Our bodies mature and we seek more enjoyment....Then slowly, as our minds are shattered by opposing obstacles, we search for explanations....We become confused....What we have accomplished, God only knows.*[96]

NORTH STATE INVOLVEMENT IN THE PACIFIC THEATER OF WAR

In the Pacific, American resolve to retake the initiative from the Japanese resulted in military officials under General Douglas MacArthur enacting an "island hopping" strategy, only attacking militarily vital islands and bypassing all other locations. Grim stories spread about Japanese resistance and their determination to "die to the last man." Such a military philosophy placed increased stress and pressure on military leaders to plan effectively and execute island assaults in an effort to minimize American casualties. In this regard, the coordination of men and supporting war materials to specific geographic destinations at specific times became vital. North State technical sergeant James Russell distinguished himself on many occasions as the Pacific front moved from New Guinea northward toward the Philippines. Already honored with two Air Medals, Russell received a bronze leaf cluster "for meritorious achievement" on numerous occasions in the South Pacific. Given the dangerous task of dropping supplies and transporting men to advanced positions in General MacArthur's offensive against Japanese units, the young North State pilot needed to fly low, sometimes very low, over mountainous, quickly rising terrain, often during inclement weather, on a few occasions landing or dropping supplies only a few miles from Japanese-held lines. The citation read, "He demonstrated outstanding ability, courage, and devotion to duty."

On July 25, Lieutenant James Culliton of Oroville climbed down off his B-24 bomber from the airstrip on the island of Okinawa, greeting his ground crew with these words: "Lots of fun today." What he really meant by "fun" involved a high-stakes encounter against eight Japanese fighter planes. Writing home, he told how his formation of Liberator bombers received orders to drop heavy ordnance bombs on Tsuiki Airfield on the northern Japanese island of Kyushu. Everything went fine until they discovered thirty Japanese fighter planes approaching immediately after they dumped their bomb load. For some reason, eight of the fighters decided to focus on Culliton's plane, zipping above and below the B-24 and firing short blasts of machine gun bursts. Fighting back, one gunner on the B-24 hit a fighter, "blasting a wing off." Culliton remembered watching the wounded fighter "burning as it passed the tail of the bomber and crashing into the water."[97] In recalling the incident, Culliton proudly declared his bombs "hit right in the target area, starting a large fire."

The Battle of the Bulge

With the coming of Christmas 1944, most Americans believed the war would be over in the early spring of 1945 as Allied troops liberated Paris and began pushing Nazis forces eastward and back to Germany. However, in a complete surprise, Hitler and his top generals planned a last-ditch effort to regain the initiative by striking at American and British lines in Belgium. The attack began on December 16, but most Americans did not learn the extent of the battle until two days later, when North State newspapers carried limited information about the German assault. In an article titled "Yanks Strike Back at Nazi Belgian Offensive," readers discovered only that large German armored units had driven forward, "bending back the lines of the fiercely struggling doughboys"; this bending of the lines resulted, later, in calling the attack the Battle of the Bulge. Strict control over battle details remained in effect as American commanders debated how to contain the situation. It appeared that the Germans were throwing in their strategic reserve army units and sending up aircraft diverted from the eastern front; this was an all-out, go-for-broke gamble.[98]

On the same day, North State residents raged over an article titled, "Germans Ruthlessly Kill Wounded Yanks." The story methodically recounted the gruesome events, quoting the words of a few survivors who had pretended to be dead. One survivor, William Summers, explained what happened:

> *We were just moving up to take over a position at the top of a hill and as we got to the road intersection, they opened up on us. They had at least 15 to 20 tanks. They disarmed us and then searched us for wristwatches and anything else they wanted. I guess we were lined up along that road for a full hour. Then they stood us all together in an open field. I thought something was wrong. As we were standing there, one German soldier moving past in a tank column less than 50 yards away, pulled out a pistol and emptied it on our fellows. Then they opened up on us from their armored cars with machine guns. We hadn't tried to run or anything. We were just standing there with our hands up and they tried to murder us.[99]*

Another survivor, Charles Appman, described lying in the mucky field, not daring to move an inch while German "noncoms" moved through the downed Americans, shooting any who moved. Finally, when most of the German units turned away, Appman and a few other Americans "jumped up and scattered for the woods. The tank opened up on us, but I don't think it got many that time." Fewer than twenty Americans survived the massacre, as reported that day. Eventually, Allied forces concentrated their military might to crush the "bulge," forcing the Germans to continue their retreat into their home country.

For many families in the North State, tragic news came knocking at the door during the weeks just before Christmas 1944, as battles became larger and more desperate. On December 19, 1944, Mrs. Paul Hoffman, still reeling from the news that her sixteen-year-old son, Theodore, had gone missing a week before, was home attempting to keep a promise to her husband, who now fought in the Pacific, by trimming their Christmas tree with her six-year-old son, Ronald. They'd finished and she had just gone to bed when her life changed forever.

[There] *came a knock at the door—a knock almost familiar now to Mrs. Hoffman; it had been heard so often, a telegram: "The Secretary of War regrets to inform you...." T/Sgt. Paul Hoffman, husband, and father of the household had been killed in action on Leyte* [Philippines].... *Thus ended 25 years, two months, and six days of faithful service in the army. Six-year-old Ronald Gene (his birthday wish exactly a month ago was: "I wish my daddy would come home") tried to comfort his mother. Theodore could have helped a lot.*

Theodore had learned, as his mother had, by previous knocks at the door, that his brothers and her sons, Corp. [Corporal] *Walter, and Pvt. Edward had been killed in action—Walter in the south Pacific and Edward in France. Now it was the father and husband. And there was the Christmas tree, unlighted. There had been such hope that Sgt. Hoffman might somehow be home for the festive day.*

Theodore had worried about his brothers and his father; of whose death he has not learned. Once before he left home—his big brothers weren't coming back either. But he was found working in Sacramento.

Mrs. Hoffman came to Marysville last July to make a home to which her husband and the other sons would return after the war. Today there were evidences of a shattered dream wherever Mrs. Hoffman trod.

As Christmas approached, everyone seemed on edge about the war reaching a climax, worrying that loved ones might not be safe. However, Mrs. William Stubbs of Marysville, who worked at Camp Beale, received good news from her husband, now incarcerated in Japan. Stubbs, a Navy Seabee, was working on a construction squad when Japanese invading forces, early in the war, captured Guam; that event occurred on December 10, 1941. For more than two years, the Stubbs family, including a mother, a son and a daughter, kept alive the hope that William lived. The teletype message read, "Season's greeting, best wishes, and love to family and friends, am well and hoping for [a] reunion soon."[100] All letters from Japan went through censorship, with many communications never delivered due to a variety of reasons. On that same day, December 23, 1944, news came to the Morris household in Marysville that their son, Wilbur, was now being held as a prisoner of war. The army communication noted that Lieutenant Morris's incarceration location was Zentauji Prison camp on the southern Japanese island of Shikoku; no other information detailed his situation.

Chapter 8

THE END OF THE WAR, 1945

On New Year's Day 1945, Adolf Hitler made it clear that despite recent German losses and continuous advancements of Soviet forces in Eastern Europe and Allied advances in the West, he promised the German people that "the end of the war will not come before 1946 unless in a German victory because Germany will never capitulate." The news, along with the already witnessed determination of the Japanese to fight on until all died, added to the worry and frustration of Americans anxious for the hostilities to end. The question became: How do you defeat an enemy that will not give up? If surrender is not an option, what could the Allied military do to change the minds of Japanese military and political leaders?

On the same day, an article declared that "Americans know that 1945 will be a tough year." Scarcities of food and dry products had increased the year before; now the OPA remained poised to tighten the "budget" even more stringently. To North State citizens, it appeared difficult to accept the idea, as per the government, that food rationing needed to continue, with more demands on local consumers; however, readers learned that a huge humanitarian crisis now arose in overseas areas recently liberated, where surviving populations needed food and medical supplies. Inflationary pressures also provided much of the concern, along with price ceilings and rent ceilings that seemed too high. The official governmental word went out to "hold the line."[101] Good news for farmers did come out at this time, which included a 10 percent gain in "cash income" for 1944, with expectations of the same for 1945 or until the war ended.

THE BEGINNING OF THE END

As the early months of 1945 carried on, news on all fronts remained positive but with continued stiff resistance from the enemy on both fronts, Europe and the Pacific. Local military men, some of them, came home briefly on furloughs after extensive combat stints. One of these veterans, Technical Sergeant Raymond Rice, from the Marysville area, had recently completed his sixty-sixth aerial mission as a gunner in a B-25 medium bomber, spending fifteen months flying sorties over much of Europe; he was one member of the first bombing raids over the Normandy beaches for the D-Day invasion. In a local interview, he commented on the extent of the destruction that Allied bombing—American by day, British by night—generated on the German war machine. He seemed particularly specific about going out on a bombing mission "just in advance of conquering Yank troops on the western front." He claimed to have hit bridges not needed by the Allies, rail yards and anything that might impede the forward movement of U.S. troops. Rice summed up the effectiveness of the bombing, clearly telling the reporter, "The whole area of the western front shows up from the air as a shattered mess." Luckily for Rice, his extended furlough from combat included a tour of duty somewhere in America, with the caveat that his skills might be needed later in the Pacific.[102]

One local newspaper announced a hopeful sign of progress on April 13, 1945, with a headline that ran, "Nazis Said Collapsing"; the column header read, "Unofficial Reports Say Yanks Are Within 16 Miles of Capital [Berlin]." This was just one day after the tragic announcement of President Franklin Roosevelt's death; the president had suffered a stroke while resting at his Warm Springs, Georgia retreat. Local reaction was quick and sincere, with one area editorial stating, "The death of our President Franklin Delano Roosevelt is a great loss to the United States of America and the people of the world." The article noted how Roosevelt had "done more for humanity" than any other living person, reminding Americans that the former president cherished his Christian faith along with his famous humor and ability to remember everyone's name. A final salute claimed that "freedom-loving people throughout the world will mourn his passing. The greatest American of our age is dead."[103]

Around the North State, expressions of grief and determination pervaded each county. Camp Beal quickly organized a "Memorial Parade" with all military personnel and invited the public to hear from speakers including General Oscar Abbott, then in command of the base. Movie theaters throughout the North State canceled movie showings for days, and public sporting events were put on hold, from high school baseball to semiprofessional sports, including the Pacific Coast Baseball League. Most churches planned special memorial services Friday and Saturday in addition to the highlighted Sunday events. The *Appeal-Democrat* ran a column titled A Letter from Home, which many residents sent to serving men and women in and out of the country. On April 14, 1945, this same column expressed in direct terms how much President Roosevelt meant to Northern California: "We have lost our president, but you have lost your commander in chief as well. He was as much a front-line soldier as each of you and until the very end he gave his all for the same things you are fighting for."[104]

Another local newspaper recalled how the late president had both friends and enemies in the North State and the nation as a result of the huge federal government intervention in peoples' lives and the overall economy of the region during the Great Depression and the early part of the war. The article admitted, "He had made mistakes, as all men do," but the writer admitted that everyone came together for winning the war effort, appreciating Roosevelt's quality of openness: "People felt they knew him." Instead of starting each speech with the typical "My fellow Americans," Roosevelt would say, "My friends."[105] In Oroville, the three o'clock newscast on April 13, 1945, shocked Butte County residents, many thinking it was a hoax. By four o'clock, high school students, hearing rumors as school let out, raced to the local newspaper office to see if the president had indeed died. Phone inquiries jammed the city call center, and by five o'clock, flags around Oroville had been lowered to half-mast. Interestingly, some residents noticed that "army command" flags remained at full mast, learning that tradition pledged not to lower flags until "[the] end of the day"; to do so "signified retreat."[106]

Finally, on May 7 and 8, 1945, the headlines in the North State rang out the good news: "War Ends in Europe." In Oroville, the fire sirens rang loud in two series of thirty blasts at six o'clock in the morning. "The sleeping town had awakened to the fact that the long-awaited day was officially here." Later that morning, Miss Pati Randolph, from the large and impressive church organ at the Congregational church, played a fifteen-minute version, loudly, of "Grant to Us Peace in Our Time, Oh Lord." Schools attempted to hold class but closed early at one-thirty in the afternoon, with everyone, students and teachers, wanting to be with their families. Store owners closed up shop as people remained glued to radio updates on the surrender process and

This special edition of the *Appeal-Democrat* announced Victory in Europe or V-E Day, to the relief and thanks of all North State residents. While the fight with Japan would continue into August, the public realized the end of the war was now in sight. *From the* Appeal-Democrat.

news concerning the future return of loved ones fighting in the European theater of war. That night, churches in Oroville decided to "unite in service of prayer and meditation"; the eight o'clock event was well attended at the Congregational Church.

Regional businesses ran celebration advertisements, not to sell any particular product or service but rather simply to recognize Victory in Europe Day, VE Day. One Oroville ad thanked servicemen and women alike for contributing to the downfall of the Nazi regime, with the final note, "We hope the war will be over [in Japan] and they can come home soon." Another notice placed the same day, May 9, warned Japan of the American determination to finish the war.

> *Are you prepared, Hiro* [Hirohito]? *Every one of our boys is fully determined to bring this war to a speedy and successful conclusion through*

an all-out effort against you and your army. They're anxious to finish the job and hurry to the homes they love. That's why we're warning you to be prepared for the unlimited losses of both your men and your ships. Here we come, Hirohito, and there's no stopping us. [107]

On this same day, it was learned in the North State that some, maybe many, soldiers now serving in Europe would be sent from Italy directly to active combat in the Pacific, as Japanese resistance continued. One military official appeared to hint at the possibility that retiring military units in Italy might first be sent to the United States, raising North State families' hopes of seeing their service member for a short time before they were deployed to fight Japan. However, on the same day, May 8, newly sworn-in President Harry Truman "reluctantly" signed a new resolution calling for more draftees. Eighteen-year-old men would now be given six months of training before being sent to the Pacific war. He claimed the act "necessary for continuing the war against Japan." [108]

DROPPING THE ATOMIC BOMBS

August 6, 1945, completely surprised many North State families as they heard President Harry Truman announce from the White House the dropping of an atomic bomb on the Japanese city of Hiroshima. The *Chico Enterprise* newspaper carried a large-print headline that read, "Atomic Bomb Used!," adding a subtitle: "Most Destructive Force in History Hits Japanese." Reading on, Chico residents learned that "the bomb" exploded with a force equal to more than twenty thousand tons of TNT, "producing more than 2,000 times the blast of the most powerful bomb ever dropped before." The account was careful to note that the target, Hiroshima, was a large Japanese army base, not admitting that the epicenter of the blast occurred over a central section of the city containing over one hundred thousand citizens. Residents read that Secretary of War Henry Stimson, in an effort to justify the use of the atomic bomb, "predicted today that the atomic bomb will 'prove a tremendous aid' in shortening the war with Japan." [109]

In Marysville, the story of the atomic bomb exploded in vivid headlines— like "Atomic Bomb Loosed on Japan"—followed by a smaller subhead: "World's Most Terrible Weapon." Pressed for more information, President Truman let it be known that unless Japan surrendered unconditionally, "even greater powerful forms [of the bomb] are in development." Then he went on to speak the famous warning, "If they do not now accept our terms, they may expect a rain of ruin from the air, the like of which has never been seen on this earth." At first, there was little to no reaction mentioned in the newspaper concerning the pros or cons of using such overwhelming force. It was difficult for many people to understand the science or magnitude of the event. Pictures of the destruction were not yet available, and the military clamped down with strong censorship on reporting misinformation about the damage done to the city of Hiroshima. Little did North State residents know that American military leaders were already planning another nuclear strike to be executed in a few days, teasing that it might be Tokyo. While Japanese news sources reported "great damage," it was not clear if they understood the true nature of the attack; their leaders, the war cabinet, hesitated in making a decision, and some high-ranking members remained to continue the fight against the Americans.

One North State editorial finally addressed the atomic bomb issue, noting, "There are two ways of looking at this terrible new power. The happier view is that militaristic-minded nations no longer will dare make war and so expose themselves to annihilation.…But there's another and less comforting viewpoint…expressed by an editor colleague of mine, 'It makes me sick to my stomach to think of it. You wonder whether Man isn't getting too damned smart and won't destroy himself.'"[110] That sentiment began to spread as more news of the bomb's destruction became known. One reporter believed "we [America] had discovered the 'master key' for moving the World to a point where we put the planet definitely on the fritz."[111]

Writing in the *Appeal-Democrat* on August 6, the editor summed up the situation, seeing no other alternative for the Japanese government:

> *This is bitter tea for the imperialistic gentry of Japan whose delusions of invincibility inspired a vision of Asiatic and Pacific domination. Regardless of whether peace comes through surrender or annihilation, the future holds for Japan nothing more alluring than reduction to a third-rate nation, destined to struggle through generation after generation to expunge the ignominy of one fateful day* [Pearl Harbor].

On August 9, 1945, another series of headlines flashed across North State newspapers, announcing the dropping of a second, more powerful atomic bomb, this time on the naval support city of Nagasaki, the sprawling

Headlines from August 6, 1945. *From the* Appeal-Democrat.

urban center containing a population of 263,000 persons, including 400 Allied prisoners of war. The second piece of news, another war-ending event, noted that Russia, now at war with Japan, had invaded the northern Chinese province of Manchuria. Interestingly, no local response to either of these headlines appeared. Local articles looked to the future return of normal city government, eliminating rationing and getting loved ones home. Oroville readers did learn more about the destructive force unleashed; one local editor described the atomic bomb as so destructive that it "sears all life and leaves in its wake a fused mass of earth and steel and factories," a description surely received by North State residents in awe and fear.[112] Listing the population of Hiroshima, where the first bomb exploded on August 9, as 318,000 persons, the article's author recited a government estimate that 60 percent of the city was completely destroyed, giving North State readers an idea of the suspected number of deaths. Interestingly, as in similar North State editorials this day and for the next few days, the writer asked each resident to "interpret it [the dropping of the atomic bomb] according to his own habits and training." The next paragraph summed up some of those possible opinions:

> *To the militarist, a pennant of victory; to the physicist, a formula that worked; to the historian, an epoch; to a humanitarian, horror; to the poet, a turn in the road; to the musician, bass chords; to the dictator, a shroud; to the artist, the play of light and color against a backdrop of eternity; to the churchman, "an infernal era"; to the philosopher, a signpost; to the craftsman, skill; to the inventor, inspiration; to the lawmaker, bewilderment; to the Jap[anese], the end.[113]*

The next day, August 10, the nation waited for a Japanese reply to another plea from President Truman for the Japanese to surrender. Chico city officials moved ahead with plans to close down all stores, thinking that President Truman would announce a national holiday of celebration. Ministers worked with Chico State College officials to offer a special religious service in the school's large auditorium; throughout the day, Chico remained "tense" in hopes that Japan would surrender.

In Oroville, an editorial, recognizing the end of the war was near, worried that America's wartime industries might take too long to reconvert to peacetime production, anticipating military personnel seeking jobs. Some local worry centered on the question, "Who will be required to stay behind in Europe or Japan for post-war occupation operations?" Speaking for the Butte County area, the article noted, "Wives of a good many servicemen have been holding down jobs temporarily," suggesting those men would want those jobs in a priority rating system. On the positive side, the article foresaw future job opportunities in the North State centering on the areas of agriculture, home construction, recreation and dam building.[114] One column running in Marysville announced immediate job openings for "honorably discharged veterans." Among the open positions, cargo handlers, ticket agents, reservation agents, sheet metal workers, electrical repair experts and aviation instrument service workers held the most current opportunities.

Early returning veterans discovered that job openings appeared everywhere, and local newspaper advertisements placed by large companies enticed discharged servicemen to consider relocating permanently to large urban and suburban settlements, such as the San Francisco Bay Area. The Roos Brothers, a clothing sales company, promised retailing opportunities with the possibility of quick promotion.

AGRICULTURAL LABOR IN CRITICAL NEED

In terms of regional farm production, thousands of agricultural jobs needed immediate attention in August 1945; the current lack of farm labor was called "an emergency," and appeals were made to civilians and recently discharged veterans that "crops in the area must be saved." Huge quarter-page ads found their way into all North State newspapers and magazines. Many of these calls for workers came from and were sponsored by the *Country Gentleman*, a national organization for agriculture. According to its data, across the country and particularly in the North State, farm labor shortages rated the highest since early 1942. Now, in August 1945, with most available men absent from the area, it was vital to secure anyone to work in the fields, vineyards, orchards or canning houses. The Marysville ad declared, "Get a job—spare time, weekends, Sundays, during your vacation. Help your country feed our Armed Forces, our fighting Allies, and our civilian population."[115]

Local organizations in Yuba and Sutter Counties also raised the alarm about the need for more cannery and food processing plant workers. The Victory Food Committee not only asked for every available man and woman to consider employment, allowing the prospective employee to simply name the hours they could work—but at one point, the organization also encouraged "older boys and girls" to apply. In explaining the farming emergency, the California Packing Corporation ran an ad declaring,

> *The truth is that in 1945, we've got to can and ship more food than we did last year. Every hour is vital! Right now, in our community* [the North State area], *there is a big canning job to be done. There's no time to lose—the crops must be canned when they're ripe. You'll be paid for your work—so you can earn money and serve your country at the same time.*[116]

JAPAN SURRENDERS

With the war over in Europe, North State communities began to hear stories about specific military units, their whereabouts and summarizes of their combat experiences. Such was the case when local newspapers ran short articles informing readers concerning California's Thirteenth Armored Division, formerly stationed at Camp Beale; readers learned about the unit's current situation and past war experiences. With numerous North State men serving in the unit, local interest was piqued when residents learned the unit had several distinguished combat experiences. "We of course killed many Germans, captured over 33,000, and accepted the surrender of 50,000 Hungarian forces located in the Inn River area."[117]

On August 13, at 6:35 p.m. a false United Press (UP) wire story appeared suggesting that Japan had just surrendered. For a while, home radios loudly sounded the exciting news, only to retract their statements within a short time when United Press officials discounted the reports as not coming from their national sources. Word then spread as to who was responsible for releasing the incorrect information. FBI agents immediately began working with UP officials to investigate the electronic break-in of services.

Finally, on August 14, 1945, North State residents saw the two words they had waited for over three and a half years of personal grief and suffering: "WAR ENDS." Initially, residents felt numb, as if the news could not be true. Chico "let loose with a mild celebration late in the day as everyone thought about where and how to celebrate, deciding on a quiet, introspective time of thanksgiving, gathering at the Bidwell Bowl, the bowl sitting along Big Chico Creek."[118] When contacted, military officials at the Chico Airfield reported that they had no current plans for V-J Day celebrations. The local USO club, however, did plan for a special military dance night celebration.

In Oroville, the headline read, "Japanese Surrender," in a large but not oversized font. Interestingly, right next to the main news column explaining how B-29 bombers "deliver[ed] 'final' blows against Japan," another article talked about how the local board of supervisors rejected a bid to install insulation for the county hospital. Of more importance, on the front page, the Santa Cruz Fruit Company of Oroville ran an ad urgently requesting area women to apply for night shift work at their cannery, highlighting the ongoing shortage of agricultural workers, especially in canning.

In towns all over the North State, parties large and small erupted, with people young and old carrying on well into the night of August 14. In

Chico, one small group of soldiers stationed at the army airfield lingered in town, attempting to overcome the anguish of consuming too much alcohol. When interviewed, one soldier smiled and said, "I want a pretty girl to go out with me. Is there a pretty girl in Chico to go out with me tonight?" At least three servicemen paraded down the middle of Main Street and Broadway even as late as midnight on the Fourteenth; young children watched, "not realizing the full import of the celebration," grinning and clapping till the wee hours of the night. Confetti littered parts of downtown streets, while excited young people laid on their automobile horns or tapped out rhythmic horn beeps—the celebration spread to every small and large community in Northern California, as it did, indeed, throughout the nation.[119]

Among the celebrants, at least in Chico, an observer noted an "occasional service man with a serious, nostalgic look," no doubt wondering about what his family, located somewhere distant from the North State, might be doing at this epic moment in history, no doubt wondering also when he might return home. It was difficult for the police to enforce all the local laws on driving at the right speed and on the right side of the road, littering,

News arrived on August 14, 1945, that the Japanese had accepted the peace terms laid out by the Allied powers. Victory over Japan, or V-J Day, was officially the next day, on the fifteenth, and also recognized as September 2, 1945, when Japan formally surrendered on the USS *Missouri* battleship. *From the* Appeal-Democrat.

The start of a Victory over Japan (V-J) Day parade in Chico is seen above, as military personnel carry the flags down Broadway Street in August 1945. The Waterland-Breslauer Building (*right*) remains one of the largest buildings in the downtown area. *Nopel Collection.*

drunkenness and other "minor" infractions; it was a day and night to let it all out. The Chico police chief summed up his observations the next day, admitting, "Judging by what happened in other cities, Chico celebrated quietly and there were no serious injuries and no serious accidents. The public deserves credit."[120]

Meanwhile, in Oroville, one writer noted, "the community seemed unable to believe nearly four years of total war was actually over." Overall, the celebration appeared limited to car horn blowing, short bursts from the fire department's siren and steam "whistles" from the Western-Pacific Roundhouse and the Oroville Laundry and Dry Cleaners. There was, however, a fatal car accident and two other collisions on August 15; details were not provided. The police did report several incidents of persons firing shotguns in the downtown area. At the First National Bank, employees decided to set off the burglary alarm as an attempt to acknowledge the war's ending, only to frighten nearby residents as rushing sheriff cars arrived, sirens blaring, at the scene. People shouted from autos, and at least one person hung out of a car, continually ringing a cowbell.[121] Flags filled the streets, held by excited residents waving and shouting thanks and praise for everyone involved. In one interesting incident, "A small dog howled lustily in front of the Myer's Street Café and a little

boy passing by said, to a companion, 'See, even the dog is celebrating.'"
As a culminating celebration, rumors spread in Oroville that a small
carnival that had opened on one end of Myers Street was "the" gathering
place to be, eventually drawing in two thousand people; the management
commented that it ballooned to be the largest crowd ever assembled in
that area of town.

It was over.

EPILOGUE

Worldwide casualty statistics for World War II are staggering, with over 15 million battle deaths, 25 million wounded and civilian deaths estimated at 45 million. America, spared from a direct attack on the mainland, suffered 416,800 military deaths, reporting only 1,700 civilian war-related deaths. Compare this to the Soviet Union's fight for survival against the onslaught of the German Blitzkrieg attack, losing around 10 million military personnel and a ghastly 14 million additional civilian fatalities. The 16 million American service members participating during the conflict equaled 11 percent of the total national population. Of these service members, 350,000 were women occupying important roles overseas and around the nation. According to records, 38.8 percent of U.S. servicemen enlisted voluntarily (about 6 million men). Interestingly, California did not suffer the greatest number of military fatalities during the war; that distinction went to New Jersey (31,215), Oklahoma (26,554) and Hawaii (18,601), counting killed in action, died of wounds and missing in action.[122] California's number of World War II deaths appeared low at 4,347—an interesting statistic considering the large number of state men and women that served during the conflict.

If you are interested in seeing the official list of World War II casualties by county, you can visit the National Archives site using the search criteria "WWII Army Casualties: California"—note that these figures cover army personnel only. The listing provides the following information: name, service number, rank and death category. In the data categories, the following abbreviations are used: KIA (killed in action), DNB (died non-battle), FOD (finding of death—body not recoverable or not identified) and DOW (died of wounds). The figures below include all categories noted above.

Butte County	110	Sutter County	61
Colusa County	25	Tehama County	17
Glenn County	32	Trinity County	9
Shasta County	70	Yuba County	45

Eager service members expected to find jobs aplenty after their discharge, or they may have not considered it to be a challenge, thinking only about the immediate task of getting home and reuniting with family and friends. Recall that many of our soldiers came directly out of high school, a large number of them having never held a full-time job. While local North State authorities estimated that the postwar economy necessitated a workforce prepared to work successfully in new and evolving industries, many of those jobs related to the military or mechanized agriculture. Service-related positions offered another hopeful area of potential employment. Yet Ira Kirby, California chief of the Bureau of Business Education, noted in October from Sacramento that returning servicemen needed vocational training, training that might be different from the kind of special military training they received during the war. The bureau's idea here focused on working with high school students and returning veterans, offering "guidance, training, and placement."[123]

The training proposal sounded good, but the reality on the ground in the early months after the war's conclusion revealed that the unemployment rate stood at an incredibly low 1.2 percent, down from 9.9 in 1941. Thousands—no, hundreds of thousands—of women now held many current jobs; how would that work out? One major consideration: war-related industries slowly began to halt or limit production pending new orders from the War Department, laying off tens of thousands of women and men. On top of this, North State headlines, on October 8, 1945, confirmed a massive series of nationwide strikes as the government attempted to intervene and talk directly with United Mine Workers leader John L. Lewis. The week prior saw an organized walkout of 550,000 mineworkers; adding to this, 50,000 Ford Motor Company employees also went out on strike.[124] Closer to home, the American Federation of Labor Machinists working in the Bay Area voted to strike, demanding a 30 percent wage increase; most of these workers labored in key shipping and oil facilities. In the North State, Greyhound Bus Line employees saw their opportunity to improve their previous stagnant wages and benefits, holding out for days in tough negotiations; the *Chico Enterprise* noted the difficulties this imposed on the small communities of the north valley.

One of the quickest fields of economic recovery in the North State, consumer and business construction, exploded as returning veterans and their new spouses sought homes and/or desired to open businesses. At the end of 1945 and well into 1946, local newspapers ran job advertisements, searching for skilled carpenters, electricians, plumbers, excavation workers, concrete mixers and concrete-placement workers. In fact, all through the month of October 1945, the *Chico Enterprise* ran a large ad seeking twenty to thirty carpenters, offering $1.50 an hour (a good wage at that time), a workday limited to eight hours and "steady work for several years." The sponsoring company, the Chico Realty & Investment Company, understood that an explosive economic boom was about to burst on the scene throughout America, with plenty of prosperity to go around in California's North State.

Tire, gas and food rationing came to an end at different times between October 1945 and the end of the year. However, sugar remained rationed until June 1947; many customers found consumer products, in demand during the war, still hard to get, despite a massive turnover of the industry to a peacetime economy. The *Chico Enterprise* notified Butte County residents that "additional ration points may soon come off butter. All rationing of fats and oils may end by January 1 [1946]."[125]

Recognizing the financial needs of returning veterans and those North State residents who remained behind to support the home front, banks, such as Bank of America, offered special low interest rates for a wide variety of consumer necessities, including automobiles, washers, refrigerators, heaters and, of course, homes. The new program presented options through a customized portfolio called a Timeplan, recognizing that "everyone is planning ahead these days. America's automobile makers are planning new cars...and we will help you finance it."[126] The message, correctly predicting the future, designated that in the postwar era, everyone needed an automobile—and so it was to be.

The rural North State, proud of its commitment and hard work to support the home front, successfully transitioned into a postwar economy, albeit with new challenges and tasks to complete. With all these expected automobiles and peoples' strong desire to travel extensively, public pressure arose to improve existing roads and expand highways, connecting the many communities of the North State effectively with the growing sprawl of Sacramento and the ever-expanding communities in and around the San

Optimism ran high for all North State communities, big and small, for a relaxation of ration products, availability of new automobiles and economic prosperity. This photo of the small town of Paradise reveals the community center in 1945; the town's growth accelerated in the decades following the war, as residents sought the unique physical environment and proximity to Chico and the valley. *Merriam Library Digital Collection.*

Francisco Bay Area. In addition, pressure soon came for a major expanded highway system consisting of multiple lanes, called freeways, to connect all parts of California, north and south, and to connect the North State more effectively with Oregon and Washington.

Agriculture, historically a major economic foundation of the North State, continued to mechanize and expand as water availability came online from a variety of sources, such as Shasta and Oroville reservoirs, canals and smaller water-ditch systems. The Sacramento Valley, blessed with fertile soils and scientific approaches to crop and orchard management, today ranks high nationally among the most productive farm producers. In order of value produced for 2021, they are:

Butte County: rice, almonds, walnuts
Glenn County: almonds, rice, walnuts
Tehama County: almonds, walnuts, beef cattle
Sutter County: rice, walnuts, cling peaches
Shasta County: hay, cattle, apiary products[127]

Agricultural values increased by 14 percent in Butte County for the 1944 crop report, and rice continued to be an important component, with forty-eight thousand acres in production for a value of over $5 million. The airplane shown above is about to seed another Butte County rice field, circa 1948. *Merriam Library Digital Collection.*

If it can be proved that the perfect patriotic citizen exists, and if one could prove that previous generations had indeed shown the quality of exceptional patriotism after living through a lengthy and disastrous economic decade, and even if it turns out that these other generations did serve their country well, the contribution of the men, women and children of the World War II years certainly qualifies them as one of the greatest generations of the American experience.

Many of us living in the Sacramento Valley understand it is a special place to raise a family, enjoy the amenities of valley life and take advantage of the relatively close dramatic and dynamic natural landscapes, such as the Sierra Nevada Mountains, the Cascade Mountains, nearby lakes and reservoirs and the incomparable Pacific Ocean shoreline. The freedoms we enjoy living and working in and around this beautiful environment are, in large part, due to the ultimate sacrifices of countless men, women and children who stayed the course and won the war, at home and overseas. Thank you; your commitment, strength and endurance are remembered and honored.

NOTES

Chapter 1

1. Registering for the Selective Service became required as the age range increased by April 1943. Now, all men between the ages forty-five and sixty-five years old reported to local county courthouses or city halls to fill out the notification forms; this act, President Roosevelt declared, was part of an ongoing "national emergency." Hundreds of men, many "greying perceptibly," stood in lines at Marysville City Hall beginning early on the morning of April 25 as part of the fourth call for selective service registration. One newspaper reporter claimed that 220 older men completed the process by lunch hour. Another 225 men registered at the Marysville Veterans' Memorial Auditorium. Judge Warren Steel registered this day, announcing as he finished signing his official documents that it was his birthday—no one had the courage to ask his age. Twenty-five Chinese and twenty Hindu residents also registered on this same morning.
2. *Redding Record*, December 9, 1941.
3. Coleman, *P G and E of California*, 316.
4. Ibid.
5. In Red Bluff, officials divided the city into four civil defense zones, each headed by a designated "Senior Warden."
6. *Redding Record-Searchlight*, December 20, 1941.
7. Ibid.
8. *Redding Record-Searchlight*, December 1941.

9. Ibid.

10. *Oroville Mercury-Register*, January 2, 1942.

11. Admiral Husband Kimmel, commander of the Pacific Fleet, also had a round of golf planned that day but received notice around seven o'clock of a Japanese minisub discovered at the entrance to Pearl Harbor, then went directly to his headquarters to direct the defense of the island. Whitlock, before coming home to Oroville, did get a look at the captured Japanese minisub, describing it as "a big tin can with a hole in the side."

Chapter 2

12. Investigations revealed that the reported incidents did not involve action or deception by persons of Japanese descent.

13. *Appeal-Democrat*, December 8, 1941.

14. Ibid.

15. Densho Encyclopedia, "Marysville (Detention Facility)"; see "Newspaper." https://encyclopedia.densho.org/Marysville_(detention_facility)/#Library.

16. *Appeal-Democrat*, May 23, 1942.

17. Hiroshi Sugasawara, second interview with Tamotsu Shibutani, October 25, 1943, p. 5. The Japanese American Evacuation and Resettlement: A Digital Archive, Bancroft Library, UC Berkeley, BANC MSS 67/14c, folder T1.9931.

18. Ibid. Interestingly, Shibutani thought that the Tule Lake camp would afford a much better living environment and experience, writing, "Tule Lake sounded something like Lake Tahoe with blue water, fir trees and cool country. It sounded rather like a resort."

19. *Gridley Herald*, February 15, 1943. The article billed Nakamoto's death as "Last Japanese in County Called by Death."

20. *Madera Tribune*, May 27, 1944.

21. "Homicide in Camp," *Densho Encyclopedia*, https://encyclopedia.densho.org.

22. *Appeal-Democrat*, June 7, 1944.

23. However, rosters exist of these units as they formed, and they can be viewed at the National Archives and Records Administration (NARA). Search for "442nd Regimental Combat Team" online, then click on "Archive/Research Documents."

Chapter 3

24. Justin M. Ruhge, "History," California State Military History and Museums Program, www.militarymuseum.org/ChicoAAF.html.
25. The WAAC (Women's Army Auxiliary Corps) was the only branch of service open to Black women, with the first group inducted in July 1942.
26. It is interesting to know that later in the war, in April 1944, a Boeing Flying Fortress bomber (B-17) was named the *Yuba Avenger*, following a successful war bond drive contest.
27. *Appeal-Democrat*, July 5, 1943. Major General John B. Wogan served as the commanding officer of the Thirteenth Armored Division.
28. "Beale Air Force Base," Historic California Posts, Camp Stations and Airfields, Facebook.
29. *Appeal-Democrat*, January 1, 1945.
30. "Chico's Company G, 184th Infantry Regiment in World War II," California State Military History and Museums Program, https://www.militarymuseum.org/G-184InfRegtWWII.html.
31. "A Brief History of State Defense Forces of California," compiled by Colonel Richard Grossman, California Military Reserve, https://www.militarymuseum.org/SMR%20History.html.
32. *Gridley Herald*, January 5, 1943. During this month, California governor Earl Warren authorized a "war council" to look into reorganizing the state guard along the lines of the National Guard. The state guard, it was decided, would still "consist of men from all walks of life willing and able to serve at home in meeting emergencies, but who, because of business, age, or health considerations, could not be expected to serve elsewhere."
33. Rocca, *America's Shasta Dam*, 164.

Chapter 4

34. Fifth War Loan Drive, June 12, 1944, Joe Hehn Memorial Collection, https://archive.org/details/joe-hehn?query=Fifth+War+Loan+Drive.
35. *Appeal-Democrat*, June 4, 1942.
36. *Oroville Mercury-Register*, May 8, 1945. The same ad reminded families to preserve any surplus foods, stating that over three and a half billion quarts of food were canned or preserved through drying.
37. *Oroville Mercury-Register*, August 10, 1945.

38. Data reports from the government reveal that 75 percent of American households, in the first year of the war, made it a priority to save and deliver fats and oils to local collection centers, thinking this act helped the war effort. One recent article noted, "As the rationing of butter, lard, and meat was imposed beginning in 1943, fats became even more valuable." Braun, "Turning Bacon into Bombs."

39. *Oroville Mercury-Register*, July 6, 1943.

40. Ibid.

41. *Gridley Herald*, January 5, 1943.

42. *Appeal-Democrat*, April 3, 1944.

43. The Burbank Lockheed plant assembled the famous P-38 Lightning fighter, over ten thousand of them, making it the only combat plane that continued to be produced throughout the war. Convair became a consolidated aircraft company in 1943 with major manufacturing centered in San Diego. It was famous for producing the highly effective B-24 Liberator bomber and the PBY Catalina seaplane—which was in constant demand, as the plane could land and take off on land and water. Some four thousand PBYs were constructed by Convair. "PB" stands for "patrol bomber"; "Y" designates the company.

44. See "Contributions of Young Americans," American Red Cross.

45. *Daily News*, December 9, 1941.

46. *Appeal-Democrat*, June 4, 1942.

47. *Oroville Mercury-Register*, January 5, 1942.

48. Ibid.

49. *Oroville Mercury-Register*, January 3, 1942.

50. The OPA halted tire inspections for civilian automobiles beginning on April 20, 1944.

51. The government then used the cash for everything related to military and civilian support materials and services.

52. *Oroville Mercury-Register*, January 3, 1942.

53. *Redding Record*, February 15, 1943.

Chapter 5

54. *Appeal-Democrat*, July 14, 1942.

55. *Appeal-Democrat*, March 6, 1944.

56. Richard Gunderman, "Smoking Rates in US Have Fallen to All-Time Low, but How Did They Ever Get So High," The Conversation,

November 26, 2018, https://theconversation.com/smoking-rates-in-us-have-fallen-to-all-time-low-but-how-did-they-ever-get-so-high-107185.

57. "College Life during World War II Based on the Country's Military Needs," *Harvard Crimson*, December 7, 1956, www.thecrimson.com/article/1956/12/7/college-life-during-world-war-ii.

Chapter 6

58. For my biography on the life and times of Frank Crowe, see *America's Master Dam Builder: The Engineering Genius of Frank T. Crowe* (Redding, CA: Renown, 2007).

59. The dam originally was to be called Kennett Dam, but its name was changed early in the construction phase to Shasta, after impressive, snow-covered Mount Shasta to the north—the mountain itself being named for the Indigenous peoples of the area by early white settlers who, when they asked the Natives their name, heard a phrase they interpreted as "Shasta."

60. Rocca, *Shasta Dam Boomtowns*, 12–13.

61. Rocca, *America's Shasta Dam*, 15. Keswick Dam is the afterbay storage site for Shasta Dam.

62. "Key" personnel received C gas ration tickets, allotting them more fuel than the rest of the workforce. However, the expectation stood clear that the extra gasoline went toward completing work-related tasks, not personal driving trips.

63. Redding in particular is famous for its unrelenting summer heat: soaring temperatures over 110 degrees Fahrenheit are common, aligning, at times, with the extreme heat seen in the deserts of the American Southwest. The geographic encirclement of mountains stifles summer air movement, forming a "heat bowl" that builds in intensity in late July and August.

64. Rocca, *Shasta Dam Boomtowns*, 117–18.

65. Ibid., 118.

66. A warehouse-sized refrigeration plant constantly delivered thirty-five-degree water throughout each curing block of concrete. Engineers at first tried the fifty-degree Sacramento River water but found some blocks were curing unevenly, so they recommended a change to refrigerated water.

67. Rocca, *America's Shasta Dam*, 77.

68. Ibid., 84.

69. Ibid., 82.

70. Ibid., 85.

71. Much of Grand Coulee's power would go to the Hannover nuclear program in the state of Washington. Of course, the nuclear program remained top secret, even to Crowe and Lowry.
72. Rocca, *America's Shasta Dam*, 156.
73. Those interviews occurred in the 1980s as I researched material for my earlier books on Shasta Dam and on the Shasta Dam boomtown experience.
74. The Ruhr River Valley manufacturing region, a source for much of Germany's war-related weapons and machinery, was powered by a series of dams, earlier knocked out by British dam-busters using a unique weapon that "skipped along" the water, sank once it hit the dam, descended and exploded, rupturing the dam.
75. Fearing a repeat of Germany's aggressive actions in World Wars I and II, Allied leaders, at the Potsdam Conference in July 1945, decided to carve up Germany into four geographic zones, each zone under administrative jurisdiction of one of the Allied powers: the United States, the Soviet Union, Great Britain and France.

Chapter 7

76. *Gridley Herald*, December 26, 1941.
77. *Oroville Mercury-Register*, April 14, 1945.
78. *Oroville Mercury-Register*, June 8, 1944.
79. Ibid.
80. *Oroville Mercury-Register*, January 3, 1942.
81. *Oroville Mercury-Register*, July 3, 1943.
82. *Gridley Herald*, January 5, 1943.
83. *Gridley Herald*, January 26, 1943.
84. *Gridley Herald*, February 22, 1944.
85. *Gridley Herald*, January 5, 1943.
86. *Appeal-Democrat*, March 24, 1944.
87. Ibid.
88. *Appeal-Democrat*, June 6, 1944. Interestingly, the paper noted that all Reno gambling casinos agreed to shut down until six o'clock in the afternoon out of respect for the servicemen hitting the beaches in northern France.
89. Ibid.
90. *Appeal-Democrat*, June 7, 1944.
91. Ibid.

92. *Oroville Mercury-Register,* June 6, 1944.
93. *Oroville Mercury-Register,* June 8, 1944. Nick had an older brother, John, fighting somewhere in Europe, a recent paratrooper veteran of the Italian campaign. On the same day of this announcement, fourteen more Oroville young men received government notices to report for military service.
94. *Redding Record,* July 8, 1944.
95. Early models of the B-26 Marauder continually malfunctioned during takeoff and landing testing, forcing engineers to quickly discover and fix broken electrical and mechanical systems on the plane.
96. *Redding Record,* July 9, 1944. These types of philosophical letters home became common as the war dragged on, causalities mounted and men realized that the war would continue for months, maybe years.
97. *Oroville Mercury-Register,* August 15, 1945.
98. The author's father-in-law, Gene S. Tanno, received a Bronze Star for his action in rescuing over fifty American soldiers trapped behind enemy lines.
99. *Appeal-Democrat,* December 19, 1944.
100. *Appeal-Democrat,* December 23, 1944.

Chapter 8

101. *Appeal-Democrat,* January 1, 1945.
102. *Appeal-Democrat,* April 5, 1945. Some veterans of the European theater did receive reassignments to the Pacific war. These reassignments mainly consisted of training in rear areas as preparation for the planned invasion of the Japanese home islands.
103. *Appeal-Democrat,* April 13, 1945.
104. *Appeal-Democrat,* April 14, 1945.
105. *Oroville Mercury-Register,* April 13, 1945.
106. Ibid.
107. *Oroville Mercury-Register,* May 8, 1945.
108. May 8, 1945. The U.S. Senate had added the six-month training amendment over strong objections from the military.
109. *Chico Enterprise-Record,* August 6, 1945. Stimson reported that immediate results of the impact of the bomb were not available due to an "impenetrable cloud of dust and smoke" engulfing the entire city. This is a reference to the mushroom cloud that American observing planes saw as they quickly turned away from the blast.
110. *Chico Enterprise-Record,* August 8, 1945.

111. *Chico Enterprise-Record*, August 9, 1945.

112. *Oroville Mercury-Register*, August 9, 1945.

113. Ibid.

114. *Oroville Mercury-Register*, August 10, 1945.

115. *Appeal-Democrat*, August 6, 1945. The farming organization announced the pressing need for four million farm workers nationwide.

116. Ibid.

117. *Oroville Mercury-Register*, August 10, 1945.

118. The Bidwell Bowl now sits next to the Physical Science building at Chico State University. The amphitheater traces in origination to the Works Projects Administration (WPA) of the New Deal era.

119. *Chico Enterprise-Record*, August 15, 1945.

120. Ibid.

121. *Chico Enterprise-Record*, August 16, 1945.

Epilogue

122. See World Population Review (WWII Casualties by State), https://worldpopulationreview.com.

123. *Chico Enterprise-Record*, October 8, 1945.

124. Ibid. Many of the pay disputes in large and small businesses centered on promised pay raises and improved benefits at the successful conclusion of the war.

125. *Chico Enterprise-Record*, October 22, 1945. The Department of Agriculture came under pressure to end rationing across the board, even though officials found it difficult to formulate an early plan at the time of Japanese surrender.

126. *Chico Enterprise-Record*, October 10, 1945.

127. 2021 crop reports for each of the counties noted.

BIBLIOGRAPHY

Newspapers

Appeal-Democrat (Marysville CA), 1942–1944
Chico Enterprise-Record, December 1941–May 1945
Daily News (Red Bluff, CA), December 1941–May 1945
Gridley Herald, 1943–1945
Oroville Mercury-Register, 1941–1945
Redding Record-Searchlight, December 1941–May 1945

Books

Coleman, Charles M. *P G and E of California: The Centennial Story of Pacific Gas and Electric Company, 1852–1952*. New York: McGraw Hill, 1952.
Farmer, Aria Gridley. *The Red Bluff Navy: A Memoir of the Naval Air Transport Command FSU-9*. Personal publication, available at the Tehama County Genealogical & Historical Society.
Rocca, Al M. *America's Shasta Dam: A History of Construction, 1936–1945*. Redding, CA: Renown Publishing, 1994.
———. *Shasta Dam Boomtowns: Community Building in the New Deal Era*. Redding Museum of Art & History, 1993.

County Reports

Butte County Crop Report 1942–44

Selected Online Sources

American Red Cross. "Contributions of Young Americans." October 2022. https://www.redcross.org/about-us/who-we-are/history/contributions-young-americans.html.

Braun, Adee. "Turning Bacon into Bombs: The American Fat Salvage Committee." *Atlantic*, April 18, 2014. https://www.theatlantic.com/health/archive/2014/04/reluctantly-turning-bacon-into-bombs-during-world-war-ii/360298/.

Niiya, Brian. "Marysville (detention facility." Densho Encyclopedia. https://encyclopedia.densho.org/Marysville_(detention_facility)/.

Sundin, Sarah. "Lessons from the 1940s Woman—Be Involved!" June 15, 2015. https://www.sarahsundin.com/lessons-from-the-1940s-be-involved/.

INDEX

H

J

K

L

M

ABOUT THE AUTHOR

Al M. Rocca is professor emeritus of history and education at Simpson University in Redding, California. He has taught history at Sequoia Middle School in Redding and as an adjunct faculty member at Shasta College and California State University, Monterey Bay. In his long career, Dr. Rocca has served on numerous statewide curriculum and textbook committees for the California State Department of Education. His many publications for Arcadia include *Shasta County*, *Redding*, *Old Shasta and Shasta Lake: Boomtowns and the Building of Shasta Dam*. He is currently set to publish a major historical geography with McFarland titled, *Mapping Christopher Columbus: An Historical Geography of His Early Life to 1492*. Dr. Rocca currently lives in Chico, California.

Visit us at
www.historypress.com